Spiritual Authority and Temporal Power

in the Indian Theory of Government

Ananda K. Coomaraswamy

Spiritual Authority and Temporal Power

in the Indian Theory of Government

Edited by

Keshavram N. Iengar

Rama P. Coomaraswamy

INDIRA GANDHI NATIONAL CENTRE FOR THE ARTS
New Delhi

DK PRINTWORLD
Publishers of Indian Traditions

Cataloging in Publication Data — DK
[Courtesy: D.K. Agencies (P) Ltd. <docinfo@dkagencies.com>]

Coomaraswamy, Ananda Kentish, 1877-1947.
Spiritual authority and temporal power in the Indian theory of government / Ananda K. Coomaraswamy ; edited by Keshavram N. Iengar and Rama P. Coomaraswamy.
p. cm.
Reprint.
Includes bibliographical references (p.).
ISBN: 9788124607343

1. Political science — India — History. 2. Religion and state — India. I. Iengar, Keshavram N., 1929- II. Coomaraswamy, Rama P. III. Indira Gandhi National Centre for the Arts. IV. Title.

DDC 320.954 23

ISBN 13: 978-81-246-0734-3
First re-issued in 1993
Reprinted with fresh typesetting, 2013

Published by:
Indira Gandhi National Centre for the Arts
Central Vista, Janpath, New Delhi - 110 001
Phone : (011) 2338 8438
e-mail : kalakosa_ed@yahoo.co.in
Web : www.ignca.nic.in

and

D.K. Printworld (P) Ltd.
Regd. Office : *Vedaśrī*, F-395, Sudarshan Park
(Metro Station: Ramesh Nagar)
New Delhi – 110 015-11
Phones : (011) 2545 3975, 2546 6019; *Fax* : 2546 5926
e-mail : indology@dkprintworld.com
Web : www.dkprintworld.com

Printed by: D.K. Printworld (P) Ltd., New Delhi

Foreword

Spiritual Authority and Temporal Power in the Indian Theory of Government written in 1942 marks the final transition of Coomaraswamy from the art-historian to the philosopher and metaphysician. It heralds the last phase of A.K. Coomaraswamy's writings on a vast number of subjects ranging from figures of speech or figures of thought to Symplegades to that final quintessence of maturity "Time & Eternity".

Coomaraswamy's preoccupation with the interdependence of the sacred and the profane, the transcendental and the mundane, the spiritual and the temporal, however, is not new. He had explored this in many essays, such as, Mārgī and Deśī, now included in the volume entitled *Medieval and Oriental Theories of Art*. He pursued this concern in his studies in art history, specially in the context of Buddhist Art and Jaina Iconography. *Spiritual Authority and Temporal Power in the Indian Theory of Government* explores yet another dimension of this inter-play in the context of political theories.

To contemporary scholars of political theory, the very first sentence of the book, namely, "the whole of Indian political theory is implied and subsumed in the words of the marriage formula, 'I am That, thou art This, I am Sky, thou art Earth'" would come as a thunderbolt and yet, as reader peruses the closely argued, densely written text, richly supported with references from primary material, Coomaraswamy's assertion becomes a revelation. He draws attention to the relation of the authorizing mind or the reason to the efficient power —

that of the inner to the outer man as enunciated in the earliest text of the Indian tradition, the *R̥gveda*. The juxtaposition of Mitra, Agni and Brahmā as Divine archetypes of spiritual authority and Varuṇa and Indra of the temporal (Regnum) as also the analogy of the marriage of the *purohita* to the king unfolds the implicit as also explicit relationship of spiritual authority and temporal power. Each section also provides opportunity for comparison with other traditions, especially the Greek, thereby underlining the fact that the relationship between the spiritual authority and the temporal power was not restricted to the Indian tradition although there were many significant differences in approach.

With sharpness, Coomaraswamy identified the series of correspondences between the Sacerdotium and the Regnum. The Sacerdotium corresponds to the *Aśabda* Brahman and the Regnum to the *Śabda* Brahman. As is well known, the role of *Vāc* (speech) is primary and fundamental in the early Indian speculative thought: primacy is given to the silent and silence; the articulated *Sound* is secondary. *Anāhata* and *hata* sound are the musical counterparts. In this context, king is the voice that gives effect to the purposes of silent, inarticulated spiritual authority. Logically, the royal voice or what is done vocally, is almost the will of God.

As one reads and reflects on the deep insight of Coomaraswamy, it is clear that what is extracted out of these texts are essentials of a theory of governance, which transcends historical time and locale. Pertinently, he points out that the king is not a constitutional ruler whose actions merely reflect the wishes of a majority of the subjects or those of a secular minister; nor is he the king by virtue of social contract but a ruler by Divine Right. However, this does not imply that he is an "absolute ruler". On the contrary, the king himself is the subject of another king (we may add, "a higher king"). This is law (*dharma*), the very principle of royalty and justice. This notion differs from the theory of divine right of kingship or of the king representing or replicating God. Pertinently through a circuitous argument, Coomaraswamy returns to the original marriage-hymns. He reminds us of the Sky and the Earth, the universal parents upon whose harmonious co-operation the prosperity and the fertility of the universe depends; they are to be taken to be the norms and archetype of all marriages. Thus, the analogy of marriage between the *purohita* and the king becomes clear, for the *purohita* here represents the Sacerdotium and the king, the Regnum. The priest and the Agni are representatives of the Sky and the king of the Earth and their marriage is an insurance against privation and death of the kingdom. The two are complementary and interdependent and not one representing the other.

Coomaraswamy's volume drew response from the contemporaries — both positive and negative. His long-time associate, Professor George Sarton responded: "I have received your excessively scholarly work and have profited by it". Others, such as, Walter Shewring commented on the relevance of Coomaraswamy's work to contemporary political theory of governance. The relationship of the government and the governed, the majority to the minority, of plutocracy and democracy, and the dangers of a final divorce of temporal power or political power from spiritual authority or a higher moral order, are issues of today and not yesterday only. Coomaraswamy underpins the perennial questions of an outer social order and an inner psychical order or "He" or those empowered to govern. Through a series of analogies of ritual marriage of the priest and the king and the dimensions of the Sacerdotium and the Regnum, we are reminded that a temporal order can be sustained only if the centre of authority has its centre in a sacred–moral order.

Has this not contemporary relevance for the world today? A state of disorder, if not a chaos, is evident. These are not the consequences merely of economic imbalances, of socio-political ideologies, but, perhaps they have emerged from the man having cut asunder his inner and outer selves and his inability to relate spiritual authority or vision and the skills and structures of wielding temporal (today, political) power.

Professor Norman Brown — a most eminent Indologist — was no follower of Coomaraswamy, but, on reading this work he commented: "Order prevails only where all authority finally vests in God. If it is thought to spring from the people, then cosmic principles are reversed."

Keshavram N. Iengar, a scholar, almost a devotee of Coomaraswamy, has accomplished the very difficult job of editing this work, which is full of quotations, references from Sanskrit, Greek, Latin, Chinese sources. The Indira Gandhi National Centre for the Arts is grateful to him for having undertaken this along with the illustrious son of A.K. Coomaraswamy, Dr. Rama P. Coomaraswamy. This is the fifth volume in the series of IGNCA's programme of "Collected Works of A.K. Coomaraswamy".

Kapila Vatsyayan

List of Abbreviations

Vedic/Hindu

AA = *Aitareya Āraṇyaka*
AB = *Aitareya Brāhmaṇa*
Arthaśāstra = *Kauṭilya's Arthaśāstra*
AV = *Atharvaveda Saṁhitā*
BD = *Bṛhaddevatā*
BG = *Bhagavad-Gītā*
Br. S = *Brahma-Sūtras*
BU = *Bṛhadāraṇyaka Upaniṣad*
CU = *Chāndogya Upaniṣad*
GB = *Gopatha Brāhmaṇa*
ĪU = *Īśāvāsya Upaniṣad*
JB = *Jaiminīya Brāhmaṇa*
JUB = *Jaiminīya Upaniṣad Brāhmaṇa*
Kauṣ. Up. = *Kauṣītaki Upaniṣad*
KB = *Kauṣītaki Brāhmaṇa*
KU = *Kaṭha Upaniṣad*
Manu = *Manu Smṛti* or *Mānava Dharma Śāstra*
Mbh = *Mahābhārata*
MS = *Maitrāyaṇī Saṁhitā*
MU = *Maitrī Upaniṣad*
Muṇḍ. Up. = *Muṇḍaka Upaniṣad*
PB = *Pañcaviṁśa Brāhmaṇa*
ṚV = *Ṛgveda Saṁhitā*
ŚA = *Śāṅkhāyana Āraṇyaka*

ŚB = *Śatapatha Brāhmaṇa*
Śvet Up. = *Śvetāśvatara Upaniṣad*
TA = *Taittirīya Āraṇyaka*
TB = *Taittirīya Brāhmaṇa*
TS = *Taittirīya Saṁhitā*
TU = *Taittirīya Upaniṣad*
VP = *Viṣṇu Purāṇa*
VS = *Vājasaneyī Saṁhitā*
VyP = *Vāyu Purāṇa*

Buddhist

A = *Aṅguttara Nikāya*
D = *Dīgha Nikāya*
DA = *Sumaṅgala Vilāsini*
Dh = *Dhammapada*
J = *Jātaka*
M = *Majjhima Nikāya*
Mhv = *Mahāvaṁśa*
Mv = *Mahāvagga*
S = *Saṁyutta Nikāya*
Sn = *Sutta Nipāta*

Christian, Greek & Latin

AESCHYLUS

Suppl. = *Supplices*; Prom. = *Prometheus*

ARISTOTLE

Eth. = *Ethics*
Met. = *Metaphysics*
Pol. = *Politics*

BOETHIUS

De Consol. = *De Consolatione Philosophie*

CICERO

De div. = *De Divinatione*

De off. = *De officiis*

DANTE

Par. = *Paradiso*

EURIPIDES

Her. = *Heracles*

Hip. = *Hippolytus*

HERACLEITUS

Fr. = *Heraclitici Ephesii Reliquiae*

HERMES TRISMEGISTUS

Lib. = *Libellus*

OLD TESTAMENT

Cant. = *Canticle of Canticles* or *Song of Solomon*

PHILO JUDAEUS

Abr. = *De Abrahamo*

Fug. = *De Fuga et Inventione*

Heres. = *Quis rerum divinarum heres sit*

Mosis. = *De Vita Mosis*

Op. = *De Opificio Mundi*

Prob. = *Quod omnis probus liber sit*

Sac. = *De Sacrificiis Abelis et Caini*

Somn. = *De Somniis*

Spec. = *De Specialibus Legibus*

PHILOSTRATUS

Vit. Ap. = *De Vita Appolonius*

PINDAR

Nem. = *Nemeonikai*

PLATO

Rep. = *The Republic*

SEXTUS

Emp. = *Sextus Empiricus*

ST. THOMAS AQUINAS

Sum. Theol. = *Summa Theologica*

WITELO

Lib. = *Liber de intelligentiis*

Journals

Bib. Ind. = *Bibliotheca Indica*

HJAS = *Harvard Journal of Asiatic Studies*

HOS = *Harvard Oriental Series*

JAOS = *Journal of the American Oriental Society*

JBORS = *Journal of the Bihar and Orissa Research Society*

JISOA = *Journal of the Indian Society of Oriental Art*

JRAS = *Journal of the Royal Asiatic Society*

PTS = *Pali Text Society Translation series*

SBE = *Sacred Books of the East*

Note: Works not in the List of Abbreviations appear in the "Text" and "Notes" in full.

Spiritual Authority and Temporal Power in the Indian Theory of Government

puro vo mandram divyam suvr̥ktim prayati
yajñe agnim adhvare dadhidhvam । — R̥V VI.10.1

tasmai viśaḥ svayamevā namante
yosmin brahmā rājani pūrva eti । — R̥V IV.50.8

bhadrād abhi śreyaḥ prehi
br̥haspatiḥ puraetā te astu । — TS III.1.1.4

brahma purastān ma ugraṁ
rāṣṭram avyathyam asat । — AB VIII.I

predam brahma predaṁ kr̥atram . . .
brahmakṣatrayoḥ saṁśrityai । — AB III.11

brahma sat kṣatram ucyate । — AV X.2.23

rājan, satyam param brahma — satyaṁ saṁgatam astu te.
— Mbh I.69.25 (Poona edn.).[1] See also
Mbh. Śānti Parva, Chaps. 56 to 130
— Bhīṣma's discourses on *Rājadharma*

I

It may be said that the whole of Indian political theory is implied and subsumed in the words of the marriage formula "I am That, thou art This, I am Sky, thou art Earth", etc. addressed by the brāhmaṇa priest, the *purohita*, to the king in AB VIII.27. This being so, and as it has been pretended that these words were addressed by the king to the priest,[2] it becomes desirable, if the theory is to be understood, to establish once for all that, as is explicitly stated by Sāyaṇa, it is the *purohita* that utters them. A comparative study of many other contexts will show, indeed, that it is inconceivable that they should have been spoken by the king, who is unquestionably the "feminine" party in the "marriage" of the Sacerdotium (*brahma*) and the Regnum (*kṣatra*).

We must premise that Mitrāvaruṇau, and likewise Indrāgnī or Indrā-bṛhaspati, are syzygies or progenitive pairs (*mithunāni*): Mitra, Agni and Bṛhaspati being on the one hand the divine archetypes of the Sacerdotium or Spiritual authority (*brahma*) and Varuṇa and Indra those of the Regnum (*kṣatra*). We shall, for the most part, make use of the brāhmaṇas, but it must not be overlooked that the institutions therein more fully described and explained are often referred to in the *Ṛgveda*. Thus in ṚV X.52.5 — "Into thy hands, O Indra, I (Agni) commit the bolt", cf. ṚV II.11.4 — "We have laid the bolt in thy hands"[3] — corresponding to the *Accipe sceptrum* (the acceptance of the sceptre) of Western rites — is the making of the king *in divinis*. The relation of authorizing mind or reason (*kratu*) to the efficient power (*dakṣa*), that of the inner to the outer man, is explicit in ṚV VIII.13.1, "Indra, at the Soma pressings, cleanses (*punīte*, Sāyaṇa *śodhayati-kathareitai*, cf. MU VI.34.5f.) the enunciative Counsel (*kratum . . . ukthyàm*); the mighty wins increase of power (*vidé vṛdhasya dakṣasaḥ*)"; cf. ṚV X.31.2 and ŚB IV.4.4.1 discussed below. In ṚV X.124.4 Agni, the sacrificial priest (*agnir brahmā . . . vidhartā*, ṚV VII.7.5) is described as "choosing" (*vṛṇānaḥ*) Indra: it is interesting to observe that already the commons play a part in this election (*viśo na rājānaṁ vṛṇānāḥ*, ib. 8, cf. AV III.4.2). The "marriage" of the *purohita* (Saptagu, Bṛhaspati) to the king is referred to in ṚV X.47.1 — "We have taken thee by the right hand",[4] spoken reproachfully with reference to Indra's arrogance and breach of the loyalty demanded by the marital relation of the Regnum to the

Sacerdotium; as in BD VII.54f. That the *purohita*, as the designation itself implies, takes precedence of the king is explicit in ṚV IV.50.7-9, "To him the people of themselves pay homage, in whose realm the Brahmā goeth first" (*yasmin brahmā rājani pūrva eti*), quoted in AB VIII.27.[5] The feudal relationship of the Regnum to the Sacerdotium is explicit in Agni's words addressed to Indra, "I in person go before thee . . . and if thou givest me my share (or due), then shalt thou through me, O Indra, perform heroic deeds" (*ayaṁ ta emi tanvā purastād — yadā mahyam dīdharo bhāgam indrādin mayā kṛṇavo vīryāṇi*. ṚV VIII.100.1).[6] In ṚV I.18.6 Sadasaspati (who must be Agni, cf. ṚV I.21.5 *sadaspatī indrāgnī*) is called "Indra's dear and lovable friend" (*priyam indrasya kāmyam*): in ṚV I.80.1 it is the Brahmā that "prospers" him (*brahmā cakāra vardhanam*), cf. Buddhist *Śākyavardhana*.

Our starting point will be ŚB IV.I.4, where the Mixta Persona of Mitrāvaruṇau is the "Counsel and the Power" (*kratūdakṣau*, and TS II.5.2.4 *dakṣakratū* [*prāṇāpānau*]) and "these are his[7] two selves" (*asyaitāv ātmanaḥ*)[8]. . . Mitra is the Counsel and Varuṇa the Power, Mitra the Sacerdotium (*brahma*) and Varuṇa the Regnum (*kṣatra*), Mitra the Knower (*abhigantṛ*) and Varuṇa the Executive (*kartṛ*).[9] Now at the beginning these two were distinct (*agre nānā*),[10] the Sacerdotium and the Regnum: then Mitra the Sacerdotium could subsist apart from Varuṇa the Regnum, but Varuṇa the Regnum could not subsist apart from Mitra the Sacerdotium.[11] Whatever deed (*karma*) Varuṇa did that was not quickened (*aprasūtam*) by Mitra the Sacerdotium, was unsuccessful (*na . . . samānṛdhe*). So Varuṇa the Regnum called upon Mitra the Sacerdotium, saying: "Turn thou unto me (*upa māvartasva*) that we may unite (*saṁsṛjāvahai*); I assign to you the precedence (*puras tvā karavai*);[12] quickened by thee (*tvat prasūtaḥ*) I shall do deeds". That is, therefore, the origin of the *purohita*'s office. . . . Whatever deed, quickened by Mitra the Sacerdotium, Varuṇa did thenceforth, succeeded (*sam — ānr̥dhe*). The choice is mutual; if either the *purohita* or the king be ill chosen by the other it is called a commingling of right and wrong (*sukr̥taṁ ca duṣkr̥taṁ ca*).[13]

The expressions *puras tvā karavai* and *tvat prasūtaḥ* imply the technical terms *purohita, purodhātr̥, rājasū* and *rājasūya*. The *purohita,* literally "one put in front", "one who takes precedence", like Agni or Br̥haspati *in divinis,* is the king's brāhmaṇa adviser and minister (*brahma khalu vai kṣatrāt pūrvam,* AB VIII.1). The *purodhātr̥* is the king himself, who appoints the *purohita* or, more literally, "puts him in front". The *devasvaḥ* are the deities — Savitr̥, Agni, Soma, Br̥haspati, Indra, Rudra, Mitra and Varuṇa — by whom the king is "quickened" through the priest who invokes them as "king-quickeners" (*rājasvaḥ*), so that "It is these gods that now quicken (*suvate*) him, and having been quickened (*sūtaḥ*) by them, he is henceforth quickened" (*śvaḥ sūyate,* ŚB V.3.3.11, 13).[14] He rules, then by "Divine Right". The Rājasūya, or alternatively Varuṇa-sava is, then, the sacrificial and initiatory ritual of the "king's quickening"; the most essential part of this rite is an "aspersion"[15] (*abhiṣeka, abhiṣecanīya*), cf. AV IV.8.1, and this corresponds to what would now be called a "coronation".[16] The "quickening" refers to the fact that the rite is both initiatory and sacrificial; the king is brought forth, new-born from the initiatory death, by the officiating priests who are, in this respect, his "fathers".[17]

"The Counsel and the Power" are the equivalents of Plato's essentials of good government, *philosophia* and *dynamis,*[18] of the Islamic "Mercy and Majesty" (*jalāl* and *ḥalāl*), in Christian theology of the spirit that giveth life and the letter that killeth (II Cor. III.6), and of our "Right and Might". "Counsel" (*kratu, kratos*) might have been rendered as "Will", in accordance with the definition in our text, ŚB IV.1.4.1, "Whenever with one's mind (*mánasā*) one wills (*kāmáyate*) anything, such as 'This I want' or 'This I would do', that is the 'counsel'", cf. R̥V X.129.4

kámas . . . mánaso rétaḥ prathamám, AV XIX.52, AA I.3.2 *manasā hi sarvān kāmān dhyāyati . . . vācā hi sarvān kāmān vadati*, and JB I.68 *mano ha vai prajāpatir devatā, so kāmayata*: or by "authority", what we have a mind to do being the authority for what we actually do. The act expresses what was willed. This being so, we see that "the counsel and the power" correspond to Philo's poetic and ordaining "God" and controlling "Lord" (see n. 7), or in other words to "his will" and "him" in Eph. I.II "the purpose of him who worketh all things after the counsel of his will". In TS V.2.3.5 where the "counsel" is the beginning of the "sacrifice" (*yajña-mukham*) and is deposited in the east (the place of origin of the *brahma*), Keith renders *kratu* by "inspiration", which is certainly a legitimate value when the application is to the individual realm, as in R̥V X.31.2 *uta svéna kratunā sám̐ vadeta, kratu* here representing the Synteresis. It is preeminently Savitr̥, Br̥haspati, the *brahma* or Brahmā (TS V.3.4.4) that "inspires" our contemplations (*dhiyo yó naḥ pracodáyāt*, R̥V III.62.10, the Gāyatrī or Sāvitrī): the priest at once inspirits and inspires the king. When the Sacerdotium and the Regnum act together, then both possess the counselling power, in R̥V I.93.5, for example, Agni and Soma are "of joint counsel" (*sákratū*), as must also be understood in the many contexts in which the Regnum (Varuṇa or Indra) are possessed of "counsel" or "counsels' powers".

Thus Manas, "mind", or rather "intellect"[19] — regularly equated with Prajāpati (TS and ŚB *passim*), and often with the breath — corresponds to *kratu*, the "counsel" and to *abhigantr̥*, the "knower": and Vāc, the "voice" — the daughter, messenger, only property and bride of Manas-Prajāpati (ŚB VIII.1.2.8, TS II.5.11.5, PB XX.14.2, AB V.23, etc.) — corresponds to *dakṣa*, the "power" and *kartr̥*, the "executive" or "agent" — "Br̥haspati is the spiritual power, Vāc the royal" (*brahma vai br̥haspatir . . . vāg vai rāṣṭrī*, AB I.19, cf. Vāc as *rāṣṭrī* in R̥V VIII.100.10 and X.125.3). The Sacerdotium as director corresponds to the *Aśabda* Brahma, and the Regnum as factor to the *Śabda* Brahma. It is with reference to the *Śabda* Brahma (the "spoken word") that it is said in JUB II.9.6 that "Vāc is the *brahma* (*mantra*), and that this air" (i.e. a vibration), and with reference to the *Aśabda* Brahma that it is said in JUB I.43.3 that "Vāc is whatever is on this side of *Brahma* (i.e. "under the Sun"), and it is taught that what is otherwhere is Brahma". Bṛhaspati, Brahmaṇaspati, the silent Brahmā, is to Vāc as is the silent to the audible Brahma. ("Brahmaṇaspati is the *Brahma*", PB XVI.5.8). She exists in him more eminently (silence is golden, speech is silver); but without her "support" no enunciation of his will is possible.

In a traditional society, whatever is said by whoever "has the say-so" is "no sooner said than done".[20] It is not with his hands but by his fiat[21] or edicts that a king works". He is the "voice" that gives effect to the purposes of the spiritual authority, and thus does the will of God on earth.[22] "What is done vocally is done indeed" (*vācā kṛtaṁ karma kṛtam, Mahānārāyaṇa Up.* IV.7). Just as *in divinis* "Indra, the Regnum, is the Voice" and it is by this voice that Agni performs the sacrifice (*karoty eva vācā . . . gamayati manasā*, JUB I.33.4), so it is at the royal sacrificer's word of command that the "work" (*karma*, the sacrificial work essential to the welfare of the kingdom) is done (ŚB I.9.1.2-3); "it is with the voice that he says 'do this', and therewith the altar is built" (ŚB X.5.1.1).[23] The dual government "knows all purposes intellectually (*manasā hi sarvān kāmān dhyāyati*) and announces them verbally" (*vācā hi sarvān kāmān vadati,* AA I.3.2). Just as the *purohita* is "preferred", so intellect takes precedence of voice (*purastād vācas . . . carati*) . . . and were it not for intellect, the voice would only babble"[24] (ŚB III.2.4.11, where for *manas* and *vāc* could be substituted *brahma* and *kṣatra*; cf. ŚB I.4.5.11); even in the ritual, whatever is uttered by a Hotṛ that has not been prompted by the Mitrāvaruṇa (Brahmā) is *asurya* (AB II.5).

We have seen that what the *purohita* "knows" (*abhigantṛ*) the king performs (*kartṛ*): in other words "the voice speaks not but what is 'known' (*abhigatam*) by intellect" (ŚB IV.6.7.10), and of this filial and wifely obedience we can say truly that "the discipline of Logos, caught up with the vision of Mythos, is a royal marriage" (L.F. Kinney, in *Journal of Philosophy*, XXXIV, 1937, p. 358).

When the royal "voice" is thus informed, "what is done vocally is done indeed" (*yad vāva vācā karoti tad etad evāsya kṛtam bhavati*, JUB II.2.8):[25] Priest and king speak "with one voice", and just as it is only when instigated (*prasūtaḥ*) by the Sacerdotium that the king is effective (ŚB IV.1.4.5), so in the same way "whatever the subject does uninstigated (*aprasūtaḥ*) by these two, the Sacerdotium and the Regnum, in misdone (*akṛtam*) and men belittle it, saying: 'Even what he does is undone' (*akṛtam*)" (AB II.38).[26] It follows from the foregoing that it is not for the king to say (command) or do anything or everything he likes, but only what is "ordered to the end" and thus "correct" (*sādhu*, ŚB V.4.4.5).[27] The king, in other words, is a *sādhaka*, whose "art" is the science of government, the "king's leading" or "policy" (*rājanīti, nīti śāstra*), in which the *purohita* has been his master: for "science" (*vidyā*, i.e. truth as distinguished from opinion) is a combination, or ensemble (*saṁhita* = *saṁdhi*), or in other words the child, of intellect and voice, both of which are essential to an enunciation of truth, and just as in the case of the macrocosmic and microcosmic harps, of which the concert (*saṁhitā*) of the player with the instrument[28] is the force (*tviṣi*), so it is only the skilled speaker that "perfects the value of the voice" (*kṛtsnam vāgarthaṁ sādhayati*), and it is especially pertinent that it is said of him who understands this doctrine of the wedding of sound and meaning that "His renown fills the earth, men hearken to him when he speaks in the assemblies, saying: "Let this be done which he desires" (ŚA VII.7, VIII.9.10, XIV). The essentially vocal character of government is well brought out in PB XII.10.4-5 where, when in the Rājasūya (quoting the text of R̥V VIII.70.1-2, "He who is the king of men, etc.") it is said: "At that very point they reach the reign of the voice (*rājyam* . . . Vācaḥ), and thereby they betake the royal sacrificer to his reign" (*rājyam evaitayā yajānaṁ gamayanti*).

This is why the king cannot be allowed to talk at random, to say what he likes, but only to speak wisely; this is why the kṣatriya, who is so much like a woman in other respects, is said to love wisdom (*paññā* = *prajñā*), where she loves ornaments (*alaṅkāra*, A III.363). For the king is only a true king in so far as he is in possession of his royal art or science, in so far as he does not fail of the end (*na hīyate arthāt*), and does not miss the mark (*sādhu bhavati, nāparādhati*); he is only a "right" (*sādhu*) ruler in so far as he is governed by his art, but "crooked" (*vr̥jina*) if he is guided not by the truth but by his own inclinations: that *ars sine scientia nihil* is as true of the art of government as of any other.

If the Oriental and traditional monarch is not a "constitutional ruler" whose actions merely reflect the wishes of a majority of his subjects or those of a secular minister, nor king by virtue of any "social" contract, but a ruler by Divine Right, this does not imply that he is an "absolute" ruler, but on the contrary that he is himself the subject of another king, as is explicit in A I.109, an echo of BU I.4.14 (*tadetat kṣatrasya kṣatram yaddharmaḥ*),[29] where it is affirmed that the law (*dharma*), than which there is nothing hither, is the very principle of royalty and justice. We see, accordingly, what ultimate value attaches to the expression "king of kings" (*adhirājo rājñām, patīnām paramam patim*, Śvet. Up. VI.7), and that while the "constitutional monarch" may be controlled by his equals, or even his inferiors, the ruler by Divine Right is controlled by a superior.

Let us consider the marriage of Indrāgnī in ŚB X.4.1.5, where Agni is expressly the Sacerdotium (*brahma*) and Indra the Regnum (*kṣatra*). They say to one another: "So long as we are thus, apart, we shall be unable to bring forth offspring; let us twain become a single form" (*ekaṁ rūpam ubhāv asāva* = *sambhavāvahai* as in JUB I.54.6 = *saha nāv astu* in PB VII.10.1), i.e. as we should say "become one flesh". Accordingly "They twain became one form"[30] (*ekaṁ rūpam ubhāv abhavatām*), that of the fire itself, and thereby brought forth offspring. The verses following (5-8) explain that in the concrete symbolism of the fire-altar, Agni is represented by the Golden Person (*puruṣa*) and Indra by the gold plate (*rukma*) that were deposited, and which represent the person in the Sun, and the solar disk itself, respectively (cf. BU II.2.2 for an analogous distinction in terms of the "pupil" and the "white" of the solar and microcosmic eyes); that Agni is represented by the "baked" (i.e. mature) material of the altar and Indra by the "unbaked" ("half-baked", immature) material, whereas when the fire is blazing this distinction disappears, the whole is "fired" and fiery (cf. "It is this Agni that he thus kindles by these two, the *brahma* and the *kṣatra*", ŚB VI.6.3.15 and X.4.1.5-9). Thus Indra becomes of one progenitive form with Agni, the form of the sacrifice itself, from which the sacrificer is to be reborn, the fire being a womb (*agnir vai devayoniḥ* AB II.14) into which the sacrificer inseminates himself (JB I.17, etc.) and from which the priest brings him to birth (*yajñād devayonyai prajanayati*, AB III.19).

The ἱερός γάμος (*hieros gamos*) is effected again in TS V.2.4 where there is union (*samiti, saṁnivapana*) of the two Agnis, viz. "Agni that was before and the one (now kindled) in the fire-pan, who hate one another" (*samanasau sacetasau arcapasau*, ŚB III.4.1.24; . . . *aviṣāte*), incidentally a very significant statement of the natural opposition of the conjoint principles. Their union is effected with the martial formula of TS IV.2.5.1

"Be ye united, of one intention, loving one another (*sámitam sáṁkalpethāṁ sampriyau*). . . I have conformed your minds, operations[31] and wills (*saṁ vām manānsi saṁ vratā saṁ u cittāny á 'karam*). . . . Be ye unanimous, sharing one home, for our sake" (*bhavataṁ naḥ sámanasau saṁokasau*), cf. ṚV V.3.2 b, X.65.8 *samokasā dyāvāpṛthivī varuṇāya savrate*, ṚV X.191.24, and AV III.8.5.[32] The last words "Be ye unanimous, etc." occur also in TS I.3.7 where they are used for the union of the fire-sticks, equated with Purūravas and Urvaśī as parents of Agni–Āyus. With this marriage of those "who hate one another", cf. ṚV X.191, and AV III.30 "Let not brother hate brother (*mā bhrātā bhrātaraṁ dviṣat* . . . an incantation (*brahma*) in virtue of which the gods are neither sundered from nor hate one another" (*na viyanti na ca vidviṣate mithaḥ*) of which the application is also to "husband and wife" (*pati, jāyā*), i.e. sky and earth, the father who separates from his daughter (ṚV X.61.6 *viyāntā*), these "two worlds" that go apart from one another (AV III.31.4 *vīmé dyāvāpṛthivī itáḥ*; TS V.1.5.8 *imau lokau vy aitām*, V.2.3.3 *dyāvāpṛthivī . . . viyatī*; AB IV.27 *tau vyaitām*; PB VII.10.1 *tau viyantau*, etc.).

This union of mutually antagonistic principles, the "former" and the "latter", i.e. elder and younger, is essentially that of Varuṇa with Mitra, for "Thou, Agni, art born as Varuṇa, and it is as Mitra that thou art kindled (ṚV V.3.1).[33] It is the former, chthonic (*purīṣya-budhnya*)[34] Agni that is Varuṇa, and "not Mitra", which is as much as to say *amitra*, "unfriend": "that which is of Mitra is not of Varuṇa" (ŚB III.2.4.18), "the Regnum takes no delight in the Sacerdotium" (ŚB XIII.1.5.2). The "two Agnis" (cf. Philo, creative and destructive ("useful") fires) are the same as those of TS V.2.7.6, AB III.4 and ŚB II.3.2.10, one whose form is that of Varuṇa and "deadly to be touched", and the other "whom one approaches, making him Mitra" (*mitrakṛtyevopāsate*).[35] They are the Agni "tied up", who as Varuṇa may attack the sacrificer, and the Agni whose "unloosing" disperses the wrath (*meni*) of Varuṇa (TS V.1.5.9, V.1.6.1). The two Agnis correspond not only to Indra and Agni, Regnum and Sacerdotium, but to the two possibilities of the Sacerdotium itself: for "the *purohita* is (originally) Agni Vaiśvānara of the five wraths" (*pañcameni*),[36] and if he be not "offered to, pacified and endeared" he repels the sacrificer "from the world of heaven, from the Regnum, might, realm and subjects", so that the king is well advised to make a Mitra, a "friend", of him — "He that is friendly with such a one, that king routs him who hates him" (*tasya rājā mitram bhavati dviṣantam apabādhate*) (AB VIII.24, 25 and 27).[37]

The marriage in JUB I.53.55 is not explicitly one of the Sacerdotium and Regnum, but of principles that are their equivalents in other contexts. The marriage is of the two worlds; referred to as "abodes" (*āyatanāni*): "In the beginning this (all) was twofold, being (*sat*) and non-being (*asat*) both. Of these two, the being is the chant, the intellect, spiration (*sāman, manas, prāṇa*); the non-being is the verse, the voice, expiration (*ṛc, vāc, apāna*). . . . She, this verse, desired intercourse (*mithunam*) with him, the chant. He asked her: 'Who art thou?' She answered: 'I am She' (*sāham asmi*). 'Then, indeed, am I He (*aham amo 'smi*)', he replied. What 'She' (*sā*) is and what 'He' (*ama*), that makes 'chant' (*sāman*), and this is the quiddity of the 'chant'.[38] 'Nay', said he, 'for thou art my sister, forsooth'." She then continues to woo her brother, who at last consents (which is, of course, the "happy ending" to the abortive wooing of Yama by Yamī in ṚV X.10).[39] When the consummation is about to take place, the well-known words of the marriage formula are uttered, "I am 'He' thou art 'She'; thou art 'She', I am 'He'. She cooperating with Me (*sāmām anuvratā bhūtvā*), let us twain generate progeny (*prajāḥ prajanayāvahai*); come, let us consort" (*ehi sambhavāvahai*).[40] They became the Virāj ("Who knoweth her *mithunatva?*", AV VIII.9.10) and "brought forth (*prājanayatām*) "Him who glows yonder" (the Sun, the

Sāma, the "Golden Person" of JUB I.48.8);[41] they ran apart (*vyadravatām* — ŚB IV.6.7.9 *vy eva dravata*), (She) saying: "He hath come into being from me" (*mad adhy abhūt*),[42] — when the expression "honey-son" (*madhu-putra*).[43] In the preceding version of JUB I.50.1-2, the "two worlds" are explicitly sky and earth, and it is the gods who call upon them to unite (*sametam*, cf. R̥V X.24.5 *abruvan devāḥ punar ā vahatād iti*), and the reluctance of the sky is his "horror" of her (*so 'sāv asyā abībhatsata*), and it is only after elaborate purifications that they unite (*sametya*, converse of *viyantā*, etc., elsewhere), and engender the solar chant.

That the marriage of the two Agnis, the former and the latter, "who hate one another", should be that of Mitra and Varuṇa is in prefect agreement with the common doctrine that Mitrāvaruṇau form a progenitive pair (*mithunam*, as in ŚB IX.5.1.54), a syzygy of conjoint principles, in which Mitra is the male and Varuṇa the female partner, an "opposition" or "polarity" which is that of day to night, of light to darkness (TB I.7.10.1 *maitraṁ vā ahaḥ vāruṇī rātriḥ*, etc.). References to Mitrāvaruṇau as *prāṇāpānau* (or *prāṇodānau*) and as *brahmakṣatrau* are too many for separate citation. More explicitly in PB XXV.10.10 and ŚB I.8.1.27 *iḍā, maitrāvaruṇī*, as also ŚB II.4.4.19 "Mitra inseminates (*retaḥ siñcati*) Varuṇa", and in ŚB IV.1.4.4 Mitra and Varuṇa "united", in ŚB XII.9.1.17 Varuṇa is the womb (*yoni*), Indra the seed (*retas*), and Savitr̥ the progenitor (*rétasaḥ prajanayitŕ̥*), an obvious allusion to the Varuṇasava and the birth of Indra; Varuṇa, in other words, being Sāvitrī, and as such the mother of the solar Indra.[44] In Mbh XII.319.39 Mitra is *puruṣa* and Varuṇa *prakr̥ti*.[45] The same relations subsist when the names of Mitrāvaruṇau are replaced by the terms *apara* and *para brahma* (*mahad-brahma, brahma-yoni*)[46] as in BG VII.5-6 and XIV.3-4 where Kr̥ṣṇa sets the embryo (*garbham*) in the Great Brahman, his own higher nature (*prakr̥tim parām*, i.e. "Natura Naturans, Creatrix Universalis, Deus"), the womb (*yoni*) of all whence is the becoming of all things, saying also that "I am the father that bestows the seed" (*bījapradaḥ pitā*). It is accordingly quite in order that so many of the terms expressing the relations of Mitrāvaruṇau, should have a sexual connotation. *Abhigantṛ*, for example, like Latin *cognoscere* and Greek γιγνώσκω (*gignosco*), Sanskrit *jñā* and English "know" ("Jacob knew his wife") has an erotic value that is even more evident in ŚB IV.6.7.10 where what is uttered by Vāc is literally a "conception" fathered by *manas* (*manasā abhigatam*). The invitation *pa māvartasva sáṁsṛjāvahai* (ŚB cited above) corresponds to the marital *mām anuvratā bhūtvā . . . sambhavāvahai* of JUB I.54.6 and the marriage formula of AV XIV.2.71, "I am He, thou art She; I am the Harmony, thou the Words; I am Sky, thou art Earth. Let us twain here become one; let us bring forth offspring" (*āmo 'hām asmi, sā tvāṁ, sāmā 'hám asmy 'ṛ́k tváṁ, dya r ahám, pṛthivī tváṁ; tāv ihá sám bhavāva, prajām ā janayāvahai*), echoed in that for the marriage of Sacerdotium and Regnum in AB VIII.27, discussed below. In the same way in ŚB X.4.1.8, in connection with the union of Sacerdotium and Regnum, here represented by Indrāgnī, *ékaṁ rūpam abhavatām . . . prājanayataḥ* corresponds to *tau virāḍ bhūtvā prajanayatām* with reference to the union of the two worlds.

Amongst the syzygies to which we have referred it is that of the two worlds, sky and earth (*dyāvāpṛthivī*, Zeus and Gaia), the universal parents upon whose harmony depend the prosperity and fertility of the entire universe, which is chiefly taken to be the norm and archetype of all marriage. Thus the *samiti* or *saṁsṛṣṭi* of *brahma* and *kṛatra* is, in the sense in which the brāhmaṇas demand in every ritual operation, a conjunction (*mithunam*) of contrasted forms, apart from which contrast there would be no effective and productive coupling. The spark of life is only evoked, the sacrificial fire is only kindled, the music only illuminated when contact has been established between two oppositely charged poles, the two ends of the "pole" that connects the altar with the sun, a pole that is "fired" from above and "lit" from below.

The relative femininity of Varuṇa will be all the more apparent if, in accordance with "the generally received opinion" (Macdonell) that Mitra is the sun and Varuṇa the (dark) sky, the solar "domain", we consider the relation of the sun (Āditya) to the sky (Dyaus): for there are many texts that refer to the sun as the husband of the sky, *pátir diváḥ*, as in AV VII.21.1 and XIII.3.4.1[47] and *dyaureva sā ādityaḥ amaḥ tatsāma*, CU I.6.3, where "He" (*ama*) is the sun and "She" (*sā*) the sky. That "the sun inseminates the sky" (*retaḥ kr̥ṇoti . . . ādityo divi,* JB II.241), that He "forms his likeness in the womb of the sky" (*sūryyo rūpáṁ kr̥ṇute dyorupásthe,* R̥V I.115.5), are no more than paraphrased in the words "Mitra inseminates Varuṇa", cited above from PB and ŚB. It is as the sun that Prajāpati unites with the sky (*ādityéna divam mithunáṁ samabhavat,* ŚB VI.1.2.4, and for Mitrāvaruṇau: *mithunaṁ . . . yena prajāyate,* ŚB II.4.4.10, 18). Dyaus is conspicuously feminine in JUB III.4.5f. where "The Great with the Great, the God with the Goddess, Brahmā with the Brāhmaṇī united" (*mahān mahyā samadhatta, devo devyā samadhatta, brahma brāhmaṇyā samadhatta*), the text (as in ŚA I.6) going on to explain that the reference is to the union of Agni, Vāyu, and Āditya with earth (*iyam eva mahī*), air (*antarikṣa*) and sky (*dyaus; brāhmaṇī* implying, of course, "daughter of Brahmā"), and the Agni, Vāyu and Āditya are the "Threefold Brahmā" (verse 11, *tad brahma vai trivr̥t*, cf. MU IV.6). To this "threefold sovereign" correspond the "threefold" (*trivr̥tam*) world of R̥V X.114.1, the "three bright" realms (*usrā . . . tisraḥ*) that Br̥haspati reveals in R̥V X.67.4 = *uṣas tisràḥ* in VIII.41.3, and the "one-syllabled" voice whose three parts, distinguished by Prajāpati, are these worlds, as explained in PB XX.14.2-5.

Dyaus is feminine in some twenty Vedic contexts: the apposition *dyaur aditiḥ* (Grassmann, "der Himmel bildlich als

Mutter" {= "heaven figured as mother"}) may be noted in X.63.3, where Aditi is the "Vāc, Aditi by name, in whom may Savitṛ quieken the law (*dhárma sāviṣat*) for us" of TS I.7.7.1. This implied equation of Dyaus with Sāvitrī (the form again implying "daughter of", cf. the relation of Varuṇa to Savitṛ in ŚB XII.9.1.17 cited above) is explicit in JUB IV.27.11-12 "The sun is Savitṛ, the sky his daughter . . . this is one coupling" (*āditya eva savitā, dyaus sāvitrī . . . tad ekam mithunam*), as likewise in ŚA I.5. Sāvitrī, "daughter of Savitṛ", is the same as the Sūryā Sāvitrī, the daughter of the sun, given to Soma the king in AB IV.7, and the Sūryā of ṚV X.85.9, who is there and in AV XIV.2 the type of all brides. In AB III.48 Sūrya is Dhātṛ (m.) and Dyaus Anumatī (Gāyatrī, f.). Savitṛ is, again, Prajāpati (*bhuvanasya prajāpatiḥ*, ṚV IV.53.2, etc.), the universal progenitor, and it is as such that he unites with his own daughter "whom some all sky and others dawn" (*divaṁ voṣásam vā*, ŚB I.7.4.1; AB III.33).[48] While as *manas* (TS VI.6.10.1, etc.) he unites with Vāc (*passim*), who is again the daughter (VS XV.38, ŚB VIII.1.2.8) as well as the mother of whom he is born (PB VII.6).[49] The sun is thus beyond any question male to the sky: {Bergaingne's "Avant tout les autres éléments mâles il faut placer le ciel lui-même" is only true with the reservation "Le mâle du ciel est le soleil" (*La religion vēdique,* I.4 and 6)}. {Bergaigne's "Before all the other male elements, we must place the sky itself" is only true with the reservation "The male of the sky is the sun" (*La religion vēdique,* I.4 and 6)} cf. ŚB I.7.2.7.[50]

One further point. The marital relation of Sacerdotium to Regnum, *in divinis,* is incestuous, for it is the marriage of the Sun with his daughter Sūryā that is reflected in Prajāpati's union as Āditya with the sky (*divam mithunaṁ samabhavat*, cited above), that the "father's" union with "his own daughter" (*svāṁ duhitaram*, ṚV X.61.7) that is referred to (as Sāyaṇa recognizes) in Prajāpati's union with "his own daughter (*svāṁ duhitaram*), whom some call sky (*divam*) and others dawn" in AB III.33; a daughter that is also Vāc, Prajāpati's "own" (*svam*, PB XX.14.2), of whom he begets the Bṛhat as his eldest son in PB VII.6,[51] he being Manas (TS II.2.11.5, ŚB IX.4.1.12, JB I.68, JUB I.33.2) and Vāc the daughter of Manas (ŚB VIII.1.2.8).[52] This is likewise the story of Yama and Yamī (ṚV X.10). Heaven and earth or as in ŚB VII.2.1.10 Agni and earth, of which the "happy ending" is related in JUB I.53-54; for the relationship of "father to daughter" is more intelligibly that of "twin brother and sister", the conjoint principle of an original syzygy, that of the *Ātman, Puruṣa, yathā strī-pumāṅsau sampariṣvaktau* in BU I.4.3. "For 'man–woman' (*androgynos* = *ardhanārī*) was then a unity in form no less than name, participating equally in both the sexes, male and female" (Plato, *Symposium*, 189E), and it is just because she reflects that "he has just produced me from himself" (*ātmana eva janaitvā*) that she protests "How now can he have intercourse with me?" (*kathaṁ nu . . . sambhavati*, BU I.4.4). The separated feminine nature is no longer innocent.[53]

The relationship of sun to sky[54] (*ādityo vai brahma dyaur brāhmaṇī*, JUB III.4.9), discussed above is the same as that of Vāyu to air and Agni to earth (which last is also that of Yama to Yamī, ŚB VII.2.1.10): the ratio is by no means peculiar to the "upper world", but to all "three worlds", and to all the pairs in any of these worlds; the relationship is "universal". As was also implied in JUB III.4.5f., cited above, the three *gandharvas* or lights, Agni, Vāyu, Āditya (the "persons" of the Vedic "Trinity" (PB VI.7.2.3), and the "Universal Lights" of the fire-altar) form with their respective domains, "lots" or "participations" (*bhakti*), earth, air and sky, three forms of dawn (*uṣas*), three progenitive pairs or syzygies (*mithunāni*, PB XX.15.2-4). The text of ṚV VII.33.7 (followed in PB ib. and JB II.241) is even more explicit: "Three foremost lights, three Aryan children, inseminate the worlds (*kṛṇvanti bhúvaneṣu rétas*), three heats (*gharmāsaḥ-gharmá,* du. + Mātariśvan in R̥V X.114.1 = *trīṅ gharmān* in AV IX.1.8) ensue the dawn (*uṣásaṁ sacante*); these the Vasiṣṭhas know full well"; cf. R̥V III.56.3 "The mighty three-faced (*tryanīkáḥ*) Bull is the husband (*patyate*), he the inseminator of the everlasting dawns" (*retodhā . . . śáśvatīnām*),[55] the "three greats" (*tisró mahīḥ*) of the preceding verse (=Iḷā, Sarasvatī, and Mahī, III.5.8); R̥V VII.101.6 "He (Parjanya), the Bull, the inseminator of the everlasting-dawns (*sá retodhā vr̥ṣabháḥ śáśvatīnām*), in whom is the spirit of all that is in motion or at rest" (*tásminn ātmá jágatas tasthúṣaś ca*); and R̥V I.115.1 where "earth, air and sky" (*dyávāpr̥thivi antárikṣam*) are filled by the solar spirit of all that moves or is at rest" (*sūrya ātmā jágatas tasthúṣaś ca*). The king of kings is thus the progenitive solar spirit, who takes the forms of Agni, Vāyu and Āditya (ŚB IX.3.1.3) in relation to the triple dominion or three dominions which are so often spoken of as dawn or dawns, and are the three worlds of earth, air and sky, the "three earths" (*pr̥thivís tisrāḥ*) of which Savitr̥ is the mover (*invati*) in R̥V IV.53.5, Savitr̥'s "three bright realms" (*trírir . . . rocanāni*) that his, the *asura*'s (*asya . . . āsurasya,* cf. R̥V III.53.1), three hero-sons (*tráyo . . . vīráḥ* = VII.33.7, *prajá āryāḥ* = I.105.5 *ami yé deváḥ*) govern in R̥V III.56.7, 8.[56]

The knowledge of the three worlds and their rulers is the "triple science" (*trayī vidyā*) of JUB II.9.7. Of the logoi (*vyāhr̥tayaḥ*, JUB I.23.6 and II.9.3; ŚA.I.5.6; MU VI.6, etc.) in which it is expressed, the briefest form is that of the well-known formula *bhur bhuvas suvaḥ*. It is precisely this knowledge of the relations of the three world-overlords to their domains that fits the *purohita* for his office (AB VIII.27); the Vasiṣṭhas, its comprehensors (R̥V VII.33.7) are the "well-indoctrinated" (*suśrivāṅsaḥ*) brāhmaṇas (JB II.241), and Vāsiṣṭhas (i.e. Agni, Br̥haspati) having been Indra's *purohita* in the beginning, one can say with TS III.5.2.1 "it is, therefore, a Vāsiṣṭha that should be made the *brahmā*", and JUB III.15.1 that "The *brahma* pertains to Vasiṣṭha . . . he is the Brahmā who is a comprehensor thereof"; and assuredly, to have understood this doctrine of the three world-overlords fully would have been to have grasped the whole theory of government. Furthermore, the king who has for a *purohita* to guard his kingdom (as its Pastor, *rāṣṭragopā*)[57] a brāhmaṇa possessed of this knowledge "dies no more"[58] (*na punar mriyate*) but lives out his life to old age (AB VIII.25),[59] also PB XXIV.19.2, XXIII.12.3, XXII.12.2.

We have seen that the triple relation of the lights to their realms[60] is really the single relationship of the light to the cosmos, and since the lights and their realms, of which Savitṛ is the prime mover, are spoken of as "three skies" (*tisro divaḥ*) and "three earths" (*pṛthivīs tisraḥ*, ṚV IV.53.5) it is clear that the relationship of the Sacerdotium to the Regnum, or that of man to woman, or that of any director to any executive, can be more briefly expressed as that of sky to earth. Thus from one point of view the sky is feminine to the sun, but from another the sky is no less male to the earth (Zeus to Gaia, Europa, Danae, etc.) and literally "Lord and Master" of earth, — Adhipati, Bhūpati, Kṣetrapati and Vāstoṣpati.[61] Thus ṚV V.63.3 (*divaspatī pṛthivyā mitrāvaruṇā*, "Ye, Mitrāvaruṇau, are (respectively) lords and husbands of sky and earth" is as much as to say, "Thou, Mitra, art Lord of Dyaus (=Varuṇa), and thou, Varuṇa (=Dyaus), art Lord of Earth". It is in just the same way that while "the Regnum is dependent upon (*anuniyuktam*) the Sacerdotium, the commons are dependent on the Regnum" (AB II.33 and Aristotle, *Metaphysics*) and that while the Sacerdotium is virile to the king and commons (PB II.8.2), the king, whose *vīrya* is analogous to Indra's, and is only properly to be regarded as a dominion (*rāṣṭra*) in so far as he generates (*prajāyate*, ŚB IX.4.1.5; cf. J.V.279 where because the king has no son the people complain that the kingdom will utterly perish), is preeminently virile to the realm; so that while the virility (*vīrya*) pertains more eminently to the *brahma*, both *brahma* and *kṣatra* are "virilities" (ŚB I.3.5.4-5). In the same way, too, the delegation of the sceptre, the *vajra*, as the token of dominion (ŚB XIII.4.4.1), by the priest to the king, though it strengthens him with respect to his enemies, weakens him with respect to the Sacerdotium, just as when the king himself delegates authority to others they become his vassals (ṚV IV.4.15). The people are subject to the king, but not so the brāhmaṇas, "whose king is Soma" (ŚB V.4.2.3); the people are "food" for the king, but the king is "food" for the brāhmaṇa (Kauṣ Up. II.9); while there is another for whom the Regnum and the Sacerdotium both are "food" (KU II.25). There is one, Bhaga (=Āditya), "to whom even the king says: 'Apportion me a portion'" (AV III.16.2). The Regnum is not its own principle, but is controlled by another, the eternal law, the truth (*dharma, satyam*), the "kingship of the kingship" (*kṣatrasya kṣatram*, BU I.4.14). This, incidentally, provides the sanction for the well-known Cambodian doctrine of the Dharmarāja, as the real and persistent royalty, to be clearly distinguished from the king's own temporal personality: cf. "Le roi est mort, vive le roi". Even a righteous emperor is not without an overlord; and "Who is this king above the king? The eternal law" (*ko pana . . . raññ . . . rājā? dhammo*, A I.109), a law that equally rules the sage (*anudhammacārī na hīyati saccaparakkamo muni*, A I.149) and as is the king to his vassals, so are these to their own followers, so is the patron to the artist and the man to the wife, each in turn a servant and a master in a feudal hierarchy stemming from the king of kings. That the king is feminine to the priest but male to his own realm is thus nothing strange, but only a special case of order. In any hierarchy, the individual is necessarily related in one way to what is above him, and in another to his own domain.

Among the syzygies to which we have referred it is, then, that of sky and earth (*dyāvāpṛthivī*), the universal parents upon whose harmonious co-operation the prosperity and the fertility of the universe depend, that is chiefly taken to be the norm and archetype of all marriage, so that in the marriage rite the man addresses the woman with the words: "I am He, thou art She, I am the Harmony, thou the Words; I am Sky, thou art Earth.[62] Let us twain here become one; let us bring forth offspring" (*amo 'hamasmi sā tvaṁ, sāmā 'hamasmi ṛk tvaṁ, dyauraham pṛthivī tvaṁ; tāviha sam bhavāva prajāṁ ā janayāvahai,* AV XIV.2.71).[63] In the same way in China, sky and earth represent respectively the male, light and active, and female, dark and passive principles, *yang* and *yin*, and it is from this existence of the macrocosmic male and female principles that the distinction of husband and wife is derived; from the marriage of sky and earth "transformation in all its various forms abundantly proceeds" (*I Ching*, Appendix, III.43.45 and VI.31). In the same *I Ching*, Appendix I (as cited by Fung Yu-lan, *History of Chinese Philosophy*, I, p. 387) we find "Because of their union, heaven (sky) and earth, though separate, have their common work, just as man and woman, though separate, have a common will", corresponding very closely to ṚV III.54.6 where sky and earth are *nānā . . . samānena kratunā samvidāne.*[64]

We are now at last in a better position to understand the mutual choice or wooing (*varaṇa*) of one another by the high-priest and the king, and to understand the marriage formula with which the alliance of their "houses" is effected in AB VIII.27. The *purohita* has been chosen as guardian, or rather pastor, of the realm (*rāṣṭragopā*), and now addressed the king with the following *mantram*, wherewith he takes him to wife: "I am That (*ama*, 'He') thou art This (*sa*);[65] thou art This, I am That, I am Sky, thou art Earth. I am the Harmony (*sāman*), thou the Words (*ṛc*).[66] Let us twain here unite our houses (*saṁvahāvahai purāṇi*).[67] Thou art the body, protect thou my body from this Great Dread" (*asmān mahābhayāt . . . tanvam me pāhi . . . tanvaḥ soma gopāḥ,* ṚV VIII.48.9).[68]

That these words, to which Sāyaṇa refers as the *rājñaḥ purohitavaraṇa-mantram*,[69] could only have been spoken by the *purohita* to the king may be said to have been proved by the already accumulated evidence of the masculinity of the Sacerdotium with respect to the Regnum. That *amo 'ham asmi* must have been spoken by the priest is further confirmed by the fact that in CU V.2.6 the would-be king addresses the fire (the archetype of the *purohita*) with the words *amo nāmā 'si*, "Thy name is 'That' (or 'He')", cf. AV XIV.2.71 "*Sā* is This (Earth), *ama* is Agni". That it is the *purohita* that utters the words "I am That (or He)" is stated explicitly by Sāyaṇa (AB VIII.27, Commentary), *Bib.Ind.*, 1896, IV.288, line 8, *purohita aham amaḥ*). Sāyaṇa also makes it clear that the whole of the rest of this section, beginning *yā oṣadhī* . . . , is likewise spoken by the *purohita*, who thus consecrates the seat given to him by the king and at the same time blesses the realm. The *purohita* is the "man" and the king the "woman". Observe that it is to the king that the words "bear thou rule" (*tvaṁ vi rāja*) are addressed in AV III.4.1, and that it is with reference to a wife that the words "let her bear rule" (*vi rājatu*) are spoken in AV II.36.3.[70]

The essential purpose of the divine marriage, in which the priest and king are the representatives of sky and earth, is apotropaic of death, and especially famine (cf. BU I.2.1, *aśanāyā hi mr̥tyuḥ*).[71] The words of the text reflect the refrain *raksataṁ pr̥thivī no abhvāt* of R̥V I.185, addressed to sky and earth, day and night. It is by means of the divine marriage and the sacrifice that death is averted from the kingdom, as we saw in n. 57citing JB II.419. The marriage is an insurance against the privation (*abhva*) of R̥V I.185, "the great dread, the uplifted bolt" (*mahadbhayaṁ vajram udyatam*) of KU VI.2, the uplifted bolt (the millstone), dreaded by sky and earth, ŚB III.9.4.18, the great fear of BG II.40, the "fear" (*bhayam*) of Taitt. Up. II.7, cf. Sn. 1033 "the great dread, the woe of this world" (*dukkham assa mahabbhayam*): just as sky and earth (where they have been reconciled) are not afraid, nor are hurt, so the *brahma* and the *kṣatra* are not afraid nor are hurt, and one says: "Be not afraid, O thou breath-of-my-life" (AV II.15.1, 4). The congress of *mitrāvaruṇau, dyāvāpṛthivī, brahma-kṣatrau* is an aversion of the "wrath" (*manyu*) of Varuṇa, or rather a conversion by which he is made a friend (Mitra).[72]

The primary expression of the "wrath" is in drought, the precursor of famine. Prior to the marital reunion of sky and earth "there was no rain, no warmth, the five folk were at variance" (*na samajānata,* AB IV.27); it is a consequence of the marriage of the *purohita* and the king that the people are unanimous (*viśaḥ saṁjānate,* AB VIII.27). So when the separation of sky and earth, the act of "creation" essential to life but also involving death, had first been effected, "The gods all wailed, and called upon the Aśvins to 'reunite them' (*púnar ā vahatāt,* ṚV X.24.5): so the gods led them together (*samanayan,* as the queen is "led" in the Aśvamedha), and coming together, they performed this divine marriage" (*saṁyantāv etaṁ devavivāhaṁ vyavahetām,* AB IV.27) and as in VS II.16 "Consent ye together (*saṁjānathām*), sky and earth; aid ye us with rain".

For if Varuṇa is, in himself, a god of drought and privation (see n. 22), on the other hand, Mitrāvaruṇau jointly are typically "rain-gods", as in ṚV V.63, 68, and 69; and if their cosmic and earthly equivalents, sky and earth, priest and king, are likewise jointly rain-givers, this too depends upon the marital association and co-operation of the contrasted principles: the king, in other words, is directly responsible for the fertility of the land; the fall of rain in due season depends upon his righteousness or default.

ŚB I.8.3.12 adds to VS II.16 cited above, "for when sky and earth consent (or 'know' one another), then indeed it rains", explaining that Mitrāvaruṇau as *prāṇāpānau* are the same as that Vāyu, the Gale, "who is the ruler in the rain" (*yó varṣásyéṣṭe*): similarly AA III.1.2 where "the conjunction (*saṁdhi*) of sky and earth is rain, Parjanya the conjoiner" (*saṁdhātṛ*); cf. ṚV VII.101.6 where Parjanya, identified with the solar *Ātman*, is the inseminator of the (three) "everlasting-dawns" (*retodhā . . . śāśvatīnām*), and Taitt. Up. I.3.2 where Vāyu is the conjoiner (*saṁdhā*) of sky and earth; just as the priest, by means of the sacrificial ritual "conjoins" (*saṁdadhāti*) earth, Vāyu, and Āditya with earth, air, and sky (ŚA I.5), which is "a coupling of three with three for progeny" (*tisrás trivṛdbhir mithunāḥ prájātyai*, TB I.2.1.8). With reference to all these marriages, and their reflection here (*tasmād idānim puruṣasya śarīrāṇi pratisaṁhitāni*, JUB III.4.6; *pravasiyān saṁ vivāham āpnoti ya evaṁ veda*, PB VII.10.4), one may well say "What God hath joined together, let not man put asunder".

Thus, while "there was no rain" so long a sky and earth were estranged, the text goes on to say that, when the marriage has been made (cf. ŚA VII.3), "they enliven (*jinvanti*) one another; with the smoke (of the sacrifice) this world enlivens that (world), with rain that (world) enlivens this" (AB IV.27); the seminal union is effected with ṚV I.159, wherewith the priest fertilizes sky and earth (*dyāvāpṛthivyo rasaṁ dadhati*, cf. *rasa* in ṚV I.105.2) and "it is upon these two, thus saturated (*rasavatyāḥ*) that these children live (*upajīvanti*) as means of subsistence" (*upajīvanīye*, ŚB IV.3.2.12).[73] So in TS III.5.2.1 "'Quicken the Sky', he says; verily, to these worlds he announces the sacrifice . . . verily he wins rain". Similarly in PB VII.10.3; and in JB I.145 where because of the separation of sky and earth "gods and men hungered[74] (*aśanāyan*): for the gods live by what is given hence, and men by what is given thence.[75] . . . 'Let us be wedded' (*vivahāvahai*), they said. . . . Yonder world thence gave the dawn to this world as a marriage gift, and this world hence the smoke[76] (of the morning sacrifice); yonder world thence gave the rain to this world as a marriage gift, and this world hence the divine service (*devayajanam*, the sacrifice to the gods) to that world." So when it rains hard all day night men say: "Earth and sky have united" (*samādhātam*, AA III.1.2).

We can understand better now the traditional and world-wide doctrine that the very life and fertility of the realm depend upon the king,[77] to whom accordingly it is said: "For our bread (*ūrjé*) art thou, for rain unto us art thou, for our paternity of offspring (*prajānām . . . ādhipatyāya; pati* here as in 'Prajāpati'), . . . for all this have we aspersed (*abhyaṣicāmahi*) thee" (ŚB IX.3.3.11 and ŚB V.2.1.2 *iyam te rāt . . .*). For unless the king fulfils his primary function as patron of the sacrifice (*yajamāna*) the circulation of the "sower of wealth (*vásor dhārā*), the limitless, inexhaustible food of the gods" that falls from the sky as rain and is returned from the earth to the sky in the smoke of the burnt-offering will be interrupted (ŚB IX.3.3.15-16):[78] that man's offerings are transmitted to the gods in the smoke of the sacrifice is, of course, implied in the fact that Agni is the missal-priest (ṚV VII.10.3 and *passim*); it is indeed in the same way that the spirit of the deceased, whose body is offered up on the funeral pyre, ascends thence.

It is, then, only when the priest and the king, the human representatives of sky and earth, God and his kingdom, are "united in the performance of the rite" (*savrate*, etc.), only when "Thy will is done on earth as it is in heaven" (implying a mimesis of the heavenly "forms", cf. AB VI.27), that there is both a giving and a taking, a taking and a giving, not indeed an equality but a true reciprocity. Peace and prosperity, and fullness, of life in every sense of the words, are the fruit of the "marriage" of the Temporal Power to the Spiritual Authority, just as they must be of the marriage of the "woman" to the "man" on whatever level of reference. For "Verily, when a mating is effected, then each achieves the other's desire"

(CU I.1.6); and in the case of the "divine mating" of the Sacerdotium and the Regnum, whether in the outer realm or within you, the desires of the two partners are for "good" here *and* hereafter. The needs of the soul and the body are to be satisfied *together.*

But, if the king co-operating with and assimilated to the higher power is thus the Father of his people, it is none the less true that satanic and deadly possibilities inhere in the Temporal Power: when the Regnum pursues its own devices, when the feminine half of the administration asserts its independence, when might presumes to rule without respect for right, when the "woman" demands her "rights", then these lethal possibilities are realized; the king and the kingdom, the family and the house, alike are destroyed and disorder (*anr̥ta*) prevails. It was by an assertion of his independence and a claim to "equal rights" that Lucifer (to be distinguished from the Lux, as the solar disc is distinguished from the "person in the sun") fell headlong from heaven and became Satan, "the enemy": and by a like paranoia that Indra, "when maddened by pride in his own heroic-power"(*svena vīryeṇa darpitaḥ*)[79] became their oppressor (*devān bādhitum ārebhe*), and could only be reawakened (*ātmānam buddhvā*, i.e. knew himself, cf. Kauṣ Up. IV.20) from his stupor by the spiritual-power, by Saptagu-Br̥haspati (BD VII.54f., R̥V X.47). We have also the case of King Soma, who oppressed Br̥haspati but was afterwards reconciled to him (ŚB IV.1.2.4), and that of Nahuṣa, who in the epic replaces Indra for a time but is ruined by his arrogance, cf. ŚB V.5.1.2 where if the king should be "intoxicated" (*úd vā ha mādyet*) by his ritual exaltation, "Let him fall down headlong" (*prá vā patet*). A self-assertion on the part of the Regnum is at the same time destructive and suicidal.[80]

In a traditional society the oppressor is excommunicated and legally deposed; this may be followed by a submission and apokatastasis, as in Indra's case and as forseen in Islam for Iblis, or by the installation of a more regular successor in whom the kingship is reborn. In an anti-traditional society, when the oppressor has been removed by a popular revolution, those who have been oppressed propose to govern in their own interests, and become oppressor in their turn. The majority oppresses the minority. The rise of a plutocracy undermines what is still in name a majority rule. The inefficiency and corruption of the plutocracy prepares the way for the seizure of power by a single proletarian who becomes a dictator, or what is called in more technical terms a tyrant, who no longer pays even lip-service to any power above his own, and even if he has "good intentions" is nevertheless "unprincipled". This caricature of monarchy in turn prepares the way for a state of disorder (*anṛta*) such as may well be realized in the world in our own times. It is, indeed, already apparent that "what we call our civilization is but a murderous machine with no conscience and no ideals" (G. La Piana in *Harvard Divinity School Bulletin*, XXXVII.27). Such is the final consequence of the divorce of the Temporal Power from the Spiritual Authority, Might from Right, Action from Contemplation.

We have so far discussed only the cosmic (*adhi-daivatam*) and political (*adhirājyam*) aspects of the science of government and with reference to the individual as a subject. But this doctrine has also a self-referent (*adhyātmam*) application; the question is not only one of a universal and a national or civic order, but also one of an internal economy. In the last analysis the man himself is the "City of God" (AV X.2.30, BU II.5.18)[81] and it can as well be said of him as of any other city that "The city can never otherwise be happy unless it is drawn by those painters who copy a divine original" (Plato, *Rep.*, 500E, cf. KU V.1). Here also, there must exist a government in which the factors of disorder must be ruled by a principle of order, if the goals of well-being in this world and the other are to be reached. That man has two selves is a universal doctrine; these are respectively natural and supernatural, the one outer and active, the subject of passions, the other inner, contemplative and serene. The problem of the internal economy by which the man's ends (*puruṣārtha*) can all be attained is one of the relationship of the psycho-physical ego to the spiritual person, the outer king to the priest within you:[82] for as Plato so often puts it, the welfare of "the entire soul and body" depends upon the unanimity of the mortal and immortal selves within you as to which shall rule.[83] That the *purohita* is the instigator and the king the agent, reflects the individual constitution in which the Inner Person is the *kārayitṛ* and the elemental self (the Outer Man) the *kartṛ* (MU III.3, Kauṣ. Up. III.8, BG XVIII.16).

These two selves of the man, who is *dvyātman* (virtually at birth and actually by a rebirth), are respectively human, born of woman, and divine, born of the sacrificial fire (JB I.17, see JAOS 19.2, p. 116; AB III.19 *yajñād devayonyai prajanayati*, etc.).[84] The two selves correspond to (are the trace of) those of Mitrāvaruṇau, Sacerdotium and Regnum (*tāv ātmanaḥ*, ŚB IV.I.4.1), and to the two natures of the Brahma, respectively mortal, concrete and vocal, and immortal, discrete and silent, etc. (BU II.3.1, MU VI.3.15, 22, 36), whereby he is *dvaitībhāva* ("of one essence and two natures", MU VII.11.8). That the inner and the outer man are the trace of the two natures, sacerdotal and the royal, *in divinis* can be shown as follows: it is as the truth or reality (*satya*) and as untruth or unreality (*anṛta*) that Brahma enters into these worlds nominally (*nāmnā*) and phenomenally (*rūpeṇa*, ŚB XI.2.3-6),[85] in other words both as affirmation (*oṁ*) and as negation (*na*, AA II.3.6); the distinction of *satya* from *anṛta* is that of the *deva*s from the *asura*s (ŚB III.9.4.1, cf. IX.5.1.12), that of *oṁ* from *na* is that of the *deva*s from others, whether men or *asura*s (AB I.16 and II.2), as, for example in ṚV I.164.19, cf. BG II.61 and Sn. 742f.;

the distinction of *satya* from *anṛta* is also precisely that of the temporarily superhuman (deified) and priestly person of the initiated sacrificer from the secular so-and-so to which he returns when the sacred operation is relinquished (ŚB I.9.3.23 with VS I.5 and II.28, cf. AB VII.24 where the king is similarly desecrated at the conclusion of the rite where he calls upon the trinity to witness that now once more "I am who I am"); and this is the distinction between the two selves of the sacrificer, one the natural man and the other the second and divine Self to which he is sacrificially reborn (JB I.17, AB III.19, etc.); while finally, just as it is by a marriage of Mitra and Varuṇa, the *deva* and the *asura*, *brahma* and *kṣatra*, that the kingdom is maintained, so it is by a marriage of truth (*satya*) to untruth (*anṛta*) that man himself is propagated and increased (*tayor mithunāt prajāyate bhūyān bhavati*, AA II.3.6, MU VII.11.8). That the relationship is thought of as that of Outer King and Inner Sage is also clear from the actual wording of the texts; e.g. ṚV X.31.2 where "one should speak according to one's own counsel, and by the intellect handle the more glorious power" (*svena kratunā saṁ vadeta śreyāṅsaṁ dakṣaṁ manasā jagṛbhyāt*) and it is obvious that *kratu* and *manas* are the interior *brahma* and the *saṁvadana* and *dakṣa* the external *kṣatra* (we say "handle" to suggest "handfasting", because the wording could also be applied to the "taking" or "marriage" of *kratu* to *vāc*, *manas* to *dakṣa*, contemplation to action), and CU VII.25.2 where the application of the political terms *svarāj* and *anyarāj* is to the man himself.

Of the two selves, one is the psycho-physical individuality (*bhūtātman, śarīra ātman, dehika ātman, jīvātman*, etc.), this man so-and-so, the other the spiritual person (*paramātman, prajñātman, jñānātman, aśarīra ātman, sarvabhūtānām ātman, vaiśvānara ātman, ātmā sarvāntaraḥ, antarātman, mahātman*, etc.), the solar *Ātman* of ṚV I.115.1 and related texts, the pneumatic Daimon (*ātmanvat yakṣa*) of AV X.2.32 and X.8.43, the "contemplative, uninveterated, ever-youthful spirit, knowing whom none is afraid of death" of AV X.8.44: in Buddhism, the one the great of fair (*mahattā, kalyāṇattā*), the other the petty or foul self (*appatuma, pāpattā*), A I.149, 249. The former is "*this* self", the latter "*that*", "yonder", or "the other" self (AA II.3.7, *ayam ātmā . . . asāv ātmā*; AA II.5 and PB V.1.4 *itara ātmā*; ŚB I.8.3.17 and 19 *itara ātmā*, and ŚB IV.3.4.5 *anyam ātmānam;* D I.34 *añño attā*). That "Self of (this mortal) self (*ātmano 'tmā*) is called its immortal guide" (*netā amṛtah*, MU VI.7, cf. ṚV V.50.1); this self is passible, "its immortal Self (*amṛto 'syā 'tmā*) as is the drop of water on the lotus leaf" (MU III.2), i.e. unattached imperturbable.

"That art thou" (*tat tvam asi*, CU VI.8.6, etc.). In other words, this outer, active, feminine and mortal self of ours subsists more eminently in and as that inner, contemplative, masculine and immortal self of ours, to which it can and should be "reduced", i.e. "led back" or "wedded" (*nīta, upanīta*).[86] Our existence (*esse*, Werden) is contingent, our consciousness of essence (*essentia*, Wesen) is valid and indefeasible, *extempore.* But our awareness of our own essence is obscured by our conviction (*abhibhūtatva* as in MU III.2) of being essentially, and not merely accidentally, "this man", so-and-so, our fond belief "that 'I' am the doer" (BG. etc., *passim*). That other, inner man, the self "that has never become anyone" (KU II.18, cf. Hermes, Asclepius II.14b, *Deus . . . nec nasci potest, nec potuit*), meanwhile remains unknown and incredible to us so long as this outer man asserts its independence, so long as "thou knowest not thyself" (Cant. I.8, *si ignoras te*): the stupified *bhūtātman* "fails to see the generous author of existence (*bhagavantam prabhum — mahātmānam*), the (real) cause of actions (*kārayitdram*, cf. JUB I.5.2, BU I.6.3, John VIII.28, etc.), within himself" (*ātmastham*, MU III.2, cf. BG XVIII.16). Thus to have forgotten what one is, "know oneself" only as a "reasoning and moral animal" (Boethius, *De Consol.*, prose VI) is the greatest of all privations. The distinction is sharply drawn in Kaus. Up. IV.20 (cf. CU VIII.7 f.) where "so long as Indra knew not this spiritual-Self (*ātman*), so long the *asuras* (the extroverted powers of the soul, cf. Śaṅkara on BU I.3.1) overcame him. . . . When he knew it, then striking down and conquering the *asuras*, he compassed the chieftaincy, autocracy and overlordship of all gods and all beings, as may he likewise do who is a comprehensor thereof."[87]

To "want" and to "will" are incompatible, the one implies a privation, the other implies an abundance: the spirit is *wissing*, but the flesh is *weak* (Math. XXVI.41, S.Th. I.20.1 ad1-distinction of passions from will); so that, as Rūmī says, "Whoso hath not surrendered will (self-will), no will (free will) hath he" (Ode XIII in Nicholson, *Shams-i-Tabrīz*). The mirage of an individual "liberty" is the direct antithesis of the dogmatic *summum bonum*, which "highest good" is indeed a liberty, but a liberty from oneself, not of oneself (the so-and-so), the freedom of those who can say with the comprehensor "'I' do nothing" (BG V.8), with Christ that "I do nothing of myself" (John VIII.28), with the Buddha that "I wander in the world, a veritable Nemo" (Sn. 455-56) and are "free as the Godhead in its non-existence" (Eckhart); "Were it not for the shackle, who would say 'I am I'?" (Rūmī, *Mathnawī*, I.2449).

To "do as one likes" is by no means synonymous with "liberty", but much rather a subjection to the "ruling passions" (*indriyāni*) that one calls "one's own".[88] Those who are dominated by their own inclinations are "free men only in name" (Plato, *Republic*, 431c). We are much more the creatures of our thoughts than their authors. The man who does not know, "*thinks*" what he likes to think. Where we ought to like what we know, we actually "know what we like", which is to say that liking and disliking are our masters, rather than our servants. There is accordingly no greater lesson to be learnt than *not* to think for oneself, but by the Self, *ātmatas* (CU

VII.26.1) — κατα λογον, (*kata logon*) analogically.

What, then, is meant by "autonomy"? In the case of a king, to rule and not be ruled by the multitude of those who should be vassals and subjects; at home, to rule and not be ruled by one's family; and within you, to rule and not be ruled by one's desires. "He whose pleasure is in the (spiritual) self, whose love-sports are with the self, he whose bridegroom is the self, and whose bliss is in the self (*ātmaratir ātma-krīḍa ātmamithuna ātmānandaḥ*) becomes autonomous (*svarāj*) and a mover-at-will (*kāmacārin*) in every world: but those whose knowledge is heterogeneous become heteronomous (*anyarāj*), and do not become movers-at-will in any world" (CU VII.25.2):[89] for "Here on earth the children of men dwell in subjection to command, since whatever it be that they desire, whether a kingdom or field (i.e. whether it be a king or any other man), it is on that very thing that they base their life" (CU VIII.1.5),[90] and "Why then", as St. Augustine exclaims, "should men venture to pride themselves on their free will before they are set free? . . . For by whom a man is overcome, to him he is assigned in slavery" (*De Spir. et. Lit*, 52, cf. MU II.1-2).[91] When this mystical union (*ātmamithunam*) of the inner and the outer man has been consummated, when the two fires that hated one another (TS V.2.4.1-2) have been made one (*ekam bhavanti*), in this affectionate, unanimous, and co-operative marriage, then it can be said that "*This* self offers itself" (*ātmānaṁ samprayacchati*)[92] to that Self, and that Self to this self. They unite with one another (*tāv anyonyam abhisambhavataḥ*). By this (earthly, feminine) form, he (the aforesaid comprehensor of Indra as overlord) unites with yonder world (*anenāha rūpeṇāmuṁ lokam abhisambhavati*)[93] and by the form with this world (AA II.3.7); thus both worlds are gained for both selves, this world without and that other within you. We say "within you" here, because it is at "world's end" that sky and earth embrace (*saṁśliṣyataḥ*, JUB I.5.5); that world's end, beyond which there is no more grieving, is at the core of our own being, and that is the wayfarer's goal.[94]

On the other hand, we are naturally at war with ourselves, and often not merely at war with "what is divine in us", but ignorant of it because of our "notion that 'I' am the doer" (*ahaṅkāra*), and so effectively "one-selfed" (*ekātman*) and "self-less" (*anātman*), although potentially possessed of both natures (*dvyātman*), this born of the flesh and that born of the spirit. Our house is divided against itself. In this state of disorder "Man's self (the tyrant) has no other foe than the self" (the legitimate king having authority): that self is a friend to the self that hath of itself vanquished itself, but a foe at war with one who lacks the self" (*anātmanaḥ . . . śatruvat*, BG VI.5,6).[95] Such a privation of self, and corresponding mortality, was the original condition of both the gods and titans: *deva*s and *asura*s were in the beginning equally *anātman*, and only Agni *amṛta* (ŚB II.2.2.8, cf. XI.1.2.12 and XI.2.3.6), and "As are men now (i.e. self-less and mortal), so were the gods in the beginning" (TS VII.4.2.1.). The gods, however, "desired: 'Let us do away with the privation (*avartim*), the evil (*pāpmānam*), death (*mṛtyum*)'" (TS VII.4.2.1.), "They longed for the world of heavenly-light" (JUB I.15.1.), the sun himself "desired: "Let me, indeed, cut off all the evil, so that I may ascend to the world of heavenly light"; he saw the sacrifice, grasped it and sacrificed therewith; thus he cut off all the evil and ascended to the world of heavenly light, and he it is that having put off the evil, now shines" (JB II.82): it was, in fact, only "by qualification" (*arhaṇā*), "by Agni's counsels" (*kratubhiḥ*), by the Sacerdotium (*brahmaṇā*) that the gods attained their immortality (ṚV X.63.4, VI.7.4; ŚB XI.2.3.6). And as did the sun, so may now the man who is a comprehensor of the sacrifice, cut off all evil and rise above himself (JB II.82): it is only in finding him-self that a man is beatified, for "All that is other than the interior self of all, other than thy self, is an affliction" (*eṣa ta ātmā sarvāntaraḥ atô anyadārtaṁ*, BU III.4.2).[96]

The answer, then to the question "Who is worthy (*arhati*) to enter into union with (pass through the midst of) that sun?" (JUB I.6.1), i.e. "to break out of the universe",[97] is that he is able, he is an *arhat*, who answer to the question "who art thou?" "I am thyself" (JUB III.1.6, Kauṣ Up. I.2, etc.): it is to him that the welcome is addressed, "Come in, O myself" (Rūmī *Mathnawī*, I.3063). But if he has not verified the words "That art thou", if he does not know who he is, but speaks of himself by his own or a family name, he is driven or dragged away from the door and excluded from the marriage (JUB III.14.2=JB I.18; Rūmī, I.3057; Cant. I.8; Math. VII.21, 23, XXV.10; Rev. XIX.9, etc.). "Woe unto him who departs from this world, not having known that imperishable" (BU III.8.10).

Thus the first and last of all man's needs is to "know himself" (*ut sciat seipsum*, Avencebrol, *Fons Vitae*, I.2): the "science of the self" (*ātmavidyā*) is the final term of all doctrine (CU IV.14.1; Śvet. Up. I.16, etc.). The ancient and timeless oracle, "Know thyself" (γνῶθι σεαυτόν) *gnōthi seauton*, re-echoes throughout the Philosophia Perennis.[98] The doctrine of the Self is thus appropriately introduced by such questions as: "Which is the Self" (*kataraḥ sa ātmā*, AA II.6, *katamá ātmā*, BU IV.3.7, MU II.1), "Who is our 'self', what is '*Brahma*'?" (*ko na āmā, kiṁ brahma*, CU V.11.1), and "In whom, when I go forth hence, shall I be going forth?" (*kasminn aham utkrānta utkrānto bhaviṣyāmi*, Praśna U VI.3), i.e. When I "give up the ghost" (Sanctus Spiritus), shall I be in that immortal spirit, or, in the words of Blake, "seiz'd and giv'n into the hands of my own selfhood?" What the answer to this last question shall be depends upon the degree of our self-knowledge now: "Whoever departs from this world without having found the spirit, there is no freedom for him" (CU VIII.1.6), but "The comprehensor of the common person of all, the comprehensor of the logos 'That is my self', *he* when he goes forth falls in with the incorporeal self, and leaves behind him the other and corporeal self" (*sarveṣām bhūtānām āntaraḥ puruṣaḥ sa ma ātmeti, vidyāl sa utkrāmann evaitam aśarīraṁ prajñātmānam abhisampadyate vijahātītaraṁ daihikam*, ŚA VIII.7); "there can be no doubting for him who is assured of this, that 'this self of mine in the heart, is Brahma; coessential with him am I (*tam . . . abhisambhavitāsmi*) when I go forth hence'" (CU III.14.4); "Who knoweth Him, knoweth himself, and is not afraid to die" (AV X.8.44). Thus the dust returns to earth and the spirit to him who gave it (Eccl. XII.7). We need only add that these doctrines of man's two selves and of their composure (*saṁdhi, samādhi*) are as much Buddhist as Brāhmanical, and as much Platonic and Christian as either of these.

The "composure" of the *yogin* in whom the habit of *samādhi* persists is in fact the same as his "self-possession", the possession *of and by* one's self in that deathlike "sleep" that is the entelechy of the beatific conjugation of the conjoint principles, Indra and Indrāṇī, described in ŚB X.5.2.11-17 in explanation of the notions "one and many, far and near": "So let the comprehensor 'sleep' (*tásmād evaṁvít svapyāt*): He who with love leadeth forth (*praṇáyati*, cf. MU VI.7 *khalv ātmano ātmā netā amr̥tākhyaḥ:* $\sqrt{}$*nī*, 'to lead, control, marry') all his children, He is verily the Breath (*prāṇáḥ*, i.e. *Ātman*, Vāyu, Prajāpati, Sūrya, Agni, *Brahma*, and here in particular Mr̥tyu) and these breaths or lives (*prāṇaḥ*, i.e. sense-powers) are his own 'subjects' (*svāḥ*, cf. VS XII.82; BU IV.4.37, etc.), and when one sleeps (*svapiti*), then these breaths, his subjects, go in unto him (*enam . . . ápiyanti*, cf. JUB I.15.8 *prāṇam apyeti . . . sarvam prāṇam abhisameti*); this 'sleep' (*svapna*) is verily 'coming into one's own' (*svāpyaya = sva-api-aya*, cf. CU VI.7.8 *svam apīta*), as it is expressed metaphysically (*ity ácakṣate parókṣam*). . . . Thus it is that He is not merely 'One' (*ékaḥ*) but also 'several' (*ékāḥ*)" — "as what is *one* in the whole, and *many* in its parts — One absolutely, and *many* accidentally" (St. Thomas Aquinas, *Sum.*

Theol. I.11.1 *ad* 2) — and thus both *akala* and *kala* (MU VI.15). Now just as in English "coming into" is "taking possession of", so here there is play on the words *apī* (*api-i*) "to go in unto" and *āp* "to take possession of", suggested by the likeness of *svāpyaya* to *svāpi* (whether *su-āpi* — "loyal intimate or ally", or *sva-āpi*, "own intimate or ally") in AB III.16 "the Maruts, those good allies, are the Breaths" (*prāṇā vai marutaḥ svāpayaḥ*), Indra's allies in the battle with Vṛtra when all other gods desert him (ib. and III.16); and by such expressions as *āptakāma* (BU IV.3.21, cf. CU I.1.6), *kāmasyāpti* (KU II.11), *sarvāpti* (Kauṣ U. III.3), and *té bráhmaṇāpuḥ áthāmṛtá āsuḥ* (ŚB XI.2.3.6). This relationship of the loyal breaths to the Breath, their first principle, can also be stated as that of the sensitive selves (the "seeing man", *cākṣusapuruṣa*, CU VIII.12.4, the "hearing man", etc.; collectively the man himself — *prāṇā u ha vāva, rājan, manuṣyasya saṁbhūtiḥ*, JUB IV.7.4, *akṣara sammānaś cakṣurmayaḥ śrotramayaś chandomayo manomayo vāṅmaya ātmā*, AA III.2.2; cf. Hermes, *Lib.* XI.2.12a) to the central Self, as in Kauṣ. U. IV.20 where on the one hand the foreknowing-self (*prajñātman*) enters into the body, and on the other "these (sensitive) selves depend on that self as retainers on their chieftain" (*tam etam ātmānam ete ātmano 'nvavasyanti yathā śreṛṭhinaṁ svāḥ*): he for them and they for him, "For thou art ours, and we are thine" (ṚV VIII.92-32).[99] It is when a man is "asleep" in the sense intended above, and more briefly in CU VI.8.1, where "what is *called* 'being asleep' is really 'coming into one's own'" (*svapitīty ācakṣate svaiṁ hy apīlo bhavati*), and it is clear that *svapna* as a technical term really means the mastery of the senses and effectively *dhyāna*, as also in BU II.1.17 where (just as in Hermes Trismegistus, *Lib.* I.1) "a man is said to be 'asleep' when he curbs the senses" (as horses are curbed),[100] and only when he is thus "asleep", that he is really empowered and really free. "When he 'sleeps' these worlds are his, then he becomes as a great king or a great brāhmaṇa; likewise he attains to the high and the low. Even as a great king, taking with him his people, so also "this man", reining in his senses, drives about in (the chariot of) his own body at will" (BU II.1.18). The only royal road to power is to become one's own master; the mastery of whatever else follows. This is the traditional "secret of government", Chinese and Platonic as much as it is Indian.

The whole point of the injunction "Let the comprehensor sleep" (*tásmad evaṁvit svapyāt*) in ŚB X.5.2.12 will be lost if we think it is opposed to the "Let him fight" (*tasmād yuddhyasva*) or "act" (*kartum arhasi*) of BG II.18 and III.21. These are no longer conflicting, but coincident imperatives for what is now the *mixta persona* of Kṛṣṇārjunau rather than the single and hesitant person of Arjuna only. The "sleep" intended is having the sense powers in hand and under one's control and thus really possessed (as is explicit in BU II.1.17), and this is the "autonomy" of the king who is free to move-at-will in his own realm (ib. 18): while the "action" intended is the activity of one whose actions are not reactions to pleasure and pain but only such as are "correct". To combine and paraphrase BG II.69 and IV.18, "He who sees inaction in action, and action in inaction, sleep in waking and waking in sleep, he is wise, he is awake, he is all in act". "Yoga is skill in works" (*karmasu kauśalam,* BG II.50 — it will be recalled that the original value of *σοφος* (*sophos*), "wise", is precisely that of *kuśala,* "expert"); the kingly art is precisely *karma-yoga,* "and it need but little of this lore to save from the great fear" (BG II.40). The *dhāraṇā, dhyāna, samādhi* of *yoga* (Christian *consideratio, contemplatio,* and *excessus* or *raptus*) are so many degrees of self-possession, consummated in a going out of or being emptied of oneself and a finding of one's real Self, which is also the "Self of the immanent Spirit: "When the rider in the (psycho-physical) vehicle is liberated from all these things with which he has been stuffed (*paripūrṇa*) and by which (sense perceptions) he has been overcome, then indeed he proceeds to union with himself" (*ātmann eva sāyujyam upaiti*, MU IV.4; cf. Plato, *Phaedo* 66C, 67A). We are thus brought back to the deepest values of "self-possession": "When thou art rid of self, then art thou self-controlled (*dīnes selbes gewaltic [your over-riding self]* — *svarājan, έγκρατη έαυτον [egrates heautou*), and self-controlled art self-possessed (*dīnes selbes eigen [your own self]*, and self-possessed possessed of God (*ist got dīn eigen [God is your very self]*) and all that he has ever made" (Eckhart, Pfeiffer, p. 598), a passage that reads like a literal translation from an Upaniṣad: *prasannātmātmani sthitvā, sukham avyayam aśnute*, MU VI.20! By the same token a deeper sense emerges in the expression "All alone by himself", in the conflict with death, in which the issue is literally one of "victory or death", we are "all alone", but "by oneself", that means side by side with our very self, *ātmanaiva sahāyena* (Manu, VI.49; *ātmasākṣī* of Suparṇādhyāya in Muṇḍ. Up. III.1.1-10), the "Inseparable Companion" of BU II.1.11 and Kauṣ. Up. IV.12).

There remains then to be effected in every man, who is still a kingdom or house divided against itself, such a marriage of selves as we have spoken of, and as in CU VII.25 and AA II.3.7. We have already alluded to the consummation of this divine marriage (*daivam mithunam, ιερος γαμος*) described in ŚB X.5.2.11-16 as the beatific union of Indra and Indrāṇī "the persons in the right and left eyes".[101] These two are respectively the king and queen on the right and on the left; what we have elsewhere called the Inner Sage and Outer King are here, then, thought of in accordance with the functional symbolism with which we are now familiar, the king and the queen; they represent in fact the *brahma* and *kṣatra*, and just as we saw in ŚB IV.1.4.1f. that the success of whatever is undertaken by either depends upon a marital consent of wills — a special case of the general principle enunciated in CU I.1.6-8 — so here the union of Indra with Indrāṇī "makes them successful (*samardhayati*). The holy marriage, the synthesis (*saṁdhi*) of the conjoint principles, immortal and mortal "selves" implied in CU VII.25.2, is even more poignantly described in BU IV.3.21:

> That is his hypermetrical form[102] from which all evil has been struck away, free of all fear. As a man embraced by a darling bride (*priyáyā striyā sampáriṣvaktaḥ*) is conscious neither of a within or without, so this man embraced by the foreknowing-spiritual-self (*prājñéānātmánā*) knows naught of a within or a without; that is verily his (real) form, in which he is possessed of his desires, the spirit being his desire, so that he is undesirous (*ātmákāmam āptákāmam akāmám*) and is excepted from sorrow.

This is manifestly a return to the primordial state of the Spiritual Person (*ātman, puruṣa*) "as it were that of a man and a woman embraced" (*yáthā strīpúmāṅsau smpárisvaktau,* BU I.4.4):

> In dem unbegrîfen der hôhen einekeit, diu alle dinge vernihter in ir selbesheit sunder sich, ist sînde ein âne underscheit. . . . Ein und ein vereinet dâ liuhtet blôz. . . . Also wirt diu sêle got in gote. — Eckhart, Pfeiffer, pp. 517, 531[103]

The man is no longer this man so-and-so, but dissolved in himself. The outer man has been "crowned and mitred above himself" (Dante, *Purgatorio* XXVII.182). It is precisely such a crowning and mitering that is ritually enacted in the Rājasūya; the king's "divinity" is not "his own", not "this man's who sits upon the throne, but that of the principle that overrules him and of which he is, not the reality, but the living image, instrument and puppet. In this experience, the outer king is merged in the life and being of the inner sage, this man in the real self, *geworden was er ist* (become what he is): the words "That are thou" have been verified; the longing, "What thou art, that may I be" has been satisfied.

Like the king's attainment of Brahmanhood (AB VII.23) and like all the sacrificial Himmelfahrten this is, of course, an experience inevitably followed by a return to oneself, the man so-and-so. But like any other marriage, the nuptial coronation rite marks the beginning of a new order, it is a new man that ascends the throne: an outer man in operation, but now the legitimate agent of a higher than his own will. As the individual is assimilated to the Self, the woman to the man, so is the Regnum to the Sacerdotium: the consorts are unanimous, so that what the one enjoins the other performs. The individual is no longer enslaved by his own desires, but has found an infallible guide and mentor in the person of the Daimon or Indwelling Spirit (*átmanvat yakṣa, antarātman*), Hegemon (*antaryāmin, netṛ*), Synteresis[104] as Shepherd and Guardian (*rāṣṭragopā, goptṛ, ārakkha devatā*) and "correction du savoir-faire" (*pramāṇa*);[105] "the Inner Sage who may be called the chaplain" within you, and to whom the *purohita*, who is the chaplin of the king's house, corresponds in the civil realm. The artist is no longer "expressing himself", but can say with Dante that "I take note, and even as He dictates within me, I set it forth" (*Purgatorio* XXIV.52), The married woman is no longer at large, but now in-charge of a kingdom, that of her household. And all of these agreements are analogous to the agreement of an emperor who makes a treaty of peace with a rebellious vassal or would-be independent ruler who, in accordance with customary Indian policy, explicit in the *Arthaśāstra*, is now restored to his throne and empowered to govern, but now as the emperor's friend. It is the same for the inner and outer man.

There is now a state of peace, where there had been one of anxiety. The composure (*samādhi*) of the outer rebel and inner leader enables the whole man to rise above the battle even while participating in it. The king is now in reality a "highness", his actions are no longer determined by the likes and dislikes of his sensitive part (*necessitits coactionis*), but inwardly instigated, and being thus strictly speaking "inspired", participate in the "infallibility" of whatever proceeds *ex cathedra,* "from the tripod of truth"; the burden of responsibility transferred to other shoulders (BG III.30 *mayi sarvāṇi karmāṇi saṁnyasya*) no longer adds to the sum of his mortality and we can say: "O King live for ever". When we speak of a king as "His Serene Highness" we are speaking precisely of the truly royal quality of self-possession by which a king, if he be really a king, is indeed "exalted".

Thus from the standpoint of Indian sociological theory and that of all traditional politics, an individual tyranny, whether that of a despot, that of an emancipated artist, or that of the self-expressive man or self-sufficient woman, effects in the long run only what is ineffectual (*akṛtāni,* "misdeeds"): all self-importance leads to the disintegration and finally the death of the body politic, collective or individual. The essence of the traditional politics amounts to this, that "self-government" (*svarāj*) depends upon self-control (*ātmasaṁyama*), rule on ruliness. One may say that this conception of government survives even in modem India, since the political victory forseen by Gandhi is assuredly one that can only be achieved by a self-conquest.

The king is such by Divine Right and Appointment, and by the same token the executive of a higher than his own will; or if he rules only by might and does his own will, he is a tyrant and must be disciplined. The same applied to the individual who, if only concerned with the good of the work to be done and not with himself, and if he thinks of "himself" only as an instrument governed by his art, is worthy of all honour, but if he asserts and seeks to express himself, worthy of all dishonour and shame.

The kingship envisaged by the Indian and traditional doctrine is thus as far removed as could be from what we mean when we speak of an "absolute monarchy" or of "individualism". The supposedly "Machiavellian" *Arthaśāstra* flatly asserts (Bk. I. Ch. VI) that only a ruler who rules himself can long rule others: "Whatever Sovereign, even one whose dominion extends to the ends of the earth, is of perverted disposition and ungoverned senses (*viruddhir vr̥ttir avaśyendriyaḥ*)[106] must quickly perish", going on to say that:

> The whole of this Science has to do with a Victory
> Over the Powers of Perception and Action.[107]

The application is to the "king", the "man of action" and "artist" in any domain whatever; there is nothing that can be truly and well done or made except by the man in whom the marriage of the Sacerdotium and the Regnum has been consummated, nor can any peace be made except by those who have made their peace with themselves.[108]

Śubham Bhavatu

Notes and References

1. i. "Make ye the divine, adorable, perfect Agni, at the progressive. uninterrupted sacrifice, your foreman (*purohita*)";

   ii. "To him in whose realm the high priest goeth foremost, the people of themselves do homage";

   iii. "Go on thy way from good to better, Bṛhaspati be thy forerunner!"

   iv. "The spiritual-authority foremost, be my dominion dread and unassailable";

   v. "Forword the spiritual-authority, forward the temporal-power" unto their union";

   vi. "*kṣatra* (the temporal-power) is vindicated through *Brahma* (the spiritual-authority)";

   vii. "Truth, O king, is the Supreme *Brahma*; be the Truth thy consort".

   Other references to kingship and government:

   "May we as *purohitas* watch over the kingship". — TS I.7.10

   For *purohita* as guardian against wrong doing, see JB III.94

   "Kings are the theatre for the manifestation of God's kingship; clerics the mirrors for God's wisdom". — *Mathnawi* VI.3174

   "Kingship is at once the greatest of human achievements, and not to be taught" — Apollonius of Tyana, *Epistle* XXXVI.

   "The art of kingship, a king eminently connected with Justice", — Philotratus, *Vit.Ap.* VI.21

   "The government of one man if it provides all round for the welfare of the community, is popular government". — Philostratus, *Vit.Ap.* V.35

   ". . . the idea of a kingly government which respects most of all the freedom of the governed". — Marcus Aurelius, *The Meditations* I.14

"I'm for Monarchy to keep us equal". — Oliver Goldsmith

"That which now calleth itself the people is unworthy of Kings". — Nietsche.

"The authority of kings is descended from Anu". — Langdon, *Semitic Myths*, p. 294.

The concept of the kingdom of God on earth depends (as Professor Buckler often reminds us) for its revelation of the inner meaning of easern kingship".

In the Old Testament, *Psalms* 87-93, lauds the "Civitas Dei", the city of God.

Philo, in *Devita Mosis* II.4 speaks of "the king as the living Law".

The true Cynic is a king "who participates in the rule of Zeus". — *Epictetus* III.22.34, 95; *Homeric Hymns* XXX.5.4

"Our customary designation for a monarchy that aims at the common advantage is 'kingship' — (but) 'tyranny' is monarchy ruling in the interest of the monarch". — Aristotle, *Politics*, Bks. III, V.

"*Tyranny* is the rule of one seeking his own interest. *Oligarchy* seeks the interests of the rich. *Democracy* seeks the interests of the poor". — St. Thomas' commentary on Aristotle's *Politics*, Bk. III-7.

"God is not a tyrant . . . but a king governing with justice (*dikaiosyn*). . . and for a king there is no fitter name than father". — Philo, *Prob.* 2.2.

" . . . ill lordship, which doth ever cut the heart of subject peoples". — Dante *Paradiso*, VIII.73.

See Plato's *Republic* 562, for the "origin of tyranny", and his *Statesman* 276, for a king that is distinguished from the tyrant; and *Republic* 455D for Royalty defined.

Heres 258 on *Genesis* XX-7 "Restore the woman to the man, because he is a prophet, and shall pray for thee; and thou shalt live". — I *Cor.* XI. 7 ". . . the woman is the *glory* of the man".

2. J. Evola, *Rivolta contra il mondo moderno*, Milan, 1934, p. 105. Evola's thesis, in his discussion of the Regnum, forces him to misinterpret

AB VIII.27. Had it not been for this, his admirable chapter "Uomo e Donna" (of which an English version was published in *Viśvabhāratī,* Februay-April 1940), applied to the true relationships of the Sacerdorium and the Regnum (approximately "Church and State"), would have acquired a greater significance. As it is, Evola's argument for the superiority of the Regnum, the active principle, to the Sacerdotium, the contemplative principle, is a concession to that very "mondo moderno" against which his polemic is directed.

His argument is as much a perversion of the Greek as it is of the Indian doctrine. In the Greek tradition the heroic kind or caste (*genos* = *jāti*), alike in the soul and the community, — "that part of our soul which is endowed with bravery (*andreia* = Skr. *vīrya*) and courage (*thumos,* Skr. √*dhū*), and which is the lover of victory" (*philonikos* = Skr. *jiṣṇu*) (Plato, *Timaeus* 70 A) — is the best part of the mortal or animal soul, superior to the appetitive and inferior to the spiritual and immortal part that lays down the law. As such its seat is in the heart, between the bowels and the head; it is the defender of the whole community; its function is to listen to the Voice (*logos*) from the Akropolis, to serve (*hyperetein*) and co-operate in battle (*symmachos einai*) with the sacred principle against the mob of the appetites (within us) or of moneyed men (in the city). The three parts of the soul (or body politic) thus evidently correspond in hierarchy to the *brahma, kṣatra,* and *viś,* respectively the Sacerdotiurn, Regnum, and Commons of the Vedic tradition (in which the śūdra is represented by the *asuras*); and there can be no possible doubt of the superiority of the sacred to the royal character.

That the Spiritual Authority, Plato's *hieron,* etc., is also the Ruler, Plato's *archōn,* etc., just as the *brahma* is "both the *brahma* and the *kṣatra*" means indeed that the Supreme Power is a royal as well as a priestly power, but quite certainly does *not* mean that the *kṣatra* considered apart from the *brahma* is itself the supreme authority or anything more than its agent and servant.

A.M. Hocart, in *Les Castes,* Paris, 1938, p. 65, repeats Evola's error, saying "Tbe man and his wife are heaven and earth, just as are the king and the priest" where he should have said "just as are the priest and the king".

3. The Bolt (*vajra*) being the most essential symbol of the kingship as a delegated power (ṚV as cited, and TS II.1.3.4, ŚB 1.2.4.1, V.4.4.15, XIII.4.4.1.2). If we also find the royal "virility" (*vīrya*) equated with

the bow (ŚB V.3.50.30), no antinomy is involved, the bow being clearly analogous to the *vajra* (both are held upright and grasped in the middle), and the arrows discharged from it corresponding to those which are actually the penetrating points of the *vajra*, from which they are derived in TS VI.1.3 and ŚB I.2.4.1. The bow is as much as the *vajra* a solar weapon; the bolt is a "shaft" of light, the arrows that the sun discharges are "shafts" of light.

4. Perhaps as a disciple, cf. ŚB XI.5.4.2 (*hastam gṛhṇati*). Also ŚB IX.2.3.3 where Indra makes Brahman, that is, Bṛhaspati, who is the Brahmā, his ally.

5. Bṛhaspati, whose identity with Agni, priest and king, is unquestioned, is "seven-mouthed" and "seven-rayed" in verse 4 of the same hymn. He is regularly the Divine Sacerdotium (*brahma*), and high priest (Brahmā) of the gods, as Indra is the Regnum (*kṣatra*). JB II.128-30 cites Indra's appointment of Bṛhaspati as *purohita*. "Agni-Bṛhaspati" as the answer to the question asked in ṚV VIII.64.7 *brahmā kastaṁ (indraṁ) saparyati*; supported by AV III.21.3 *ya indreṇa saratham . . . agnibhyo hutaṁ astu*. The verses of our hymn are quoted in AB VIII.26, describing Bṛhaspati as the archetype of the human *purohita* and *Brahmā*, who "takes after" him. [ŚB XIII.6.2.16 "Bṛhaspati truly is the Brāhman(n)]. The *Brahmā* is, of course, the infallible brāhmaṇa priest who does not take any active part in the sacrifice, at which his presence is nevertheless indispensable. Himself remaining silent, his relation to the three other brāhmaṇa officiants whose operation is active and vocal is precisely that of director to executive, he is thus Brahmaṇaspati and Vācaspati (the *brahma*, as *ṛc* being precisely the vocalized *brahma*), and protects the kingdom (AV XIX.30.3 *brahmaṇaspatim tvām indrasyāhur varma tvam rāṣṭrāni rakṣasi*). This is the explanation of "the very close connection of *brahman* with Vāc" (cf. AA I.1.1 and 1.3.8 with Keith's notes); as *akṣara* is Brahma, *so akṣarā'* (ṚV VII.15.9 and 36.7) is Vāc; this connection is nothing other than that of *manas* = Prajāpati with Vāc, or than that of Brahma with Sarasvatī-Vāc in the "later mythology". It is not altogether easy to understand why Brahmā, the God, has been regarded as the creation of the "later mythology" (Macdonell, *Vedic Mythology*, p. 118). It would rather appear that the Buddhists were essentially right in referring to Brahmā Sanatkumāra as the supreme deity of the brāhmaṇas and to Indra Sujampati as his vassal. For Bṛhaspati, who is at once the *brahma* and the Brahmā of

the gods, is certainly himself a God, and why not, then, the God Brahmā, the person of Brahmā? "Yonder gods assuredly knew that Brahmā of old" (AV XIII.2.13) (*purā brahma devā amī viduḥ*). The most that could be said is that *brahma* in ṚV is more a title than a name, and only later on becomes a name; but this changes nothing in the nature of the person to whom the name applies.

It is only the actual iconography of Brahmā that is late, as is the Buddha's. In being "lotus-born" and therefor *padmāsana*, Bṛhaspati is still the Agni sprung from the "lotus" in ṚV VI.16.13. and "Vasiṣṭha the child of Mitrāvaruṇau, the Sacerdotium (*brahma*) born of Manas and Urvasī, whom the Viśvedevāḥ supported in the lotus", ṚV VII.33.11, where the equation of Mitra with Manas and Varuṇa with Urvaśī (f.) may be remarked. Vasiṣṭha, the Sacerdotium, is assuredly the Bṛhaspati who in ṚV VIII.96.13-15 "assumes a body in the womb of Aṁśumatī" (Psyche) and enables Indra to overcome his godless foes "with Bṛhaspati as yoke-fellow" (*bṛ́haspátinā yújá*). We see now why Vasiṣṭha should be Indra's instructor (in the *virāj*, of which "he who gets the most becomes the chieftain", *śreṣṭhaḥ*), and why formerly none but a Vāsiṣṭha (descendant of Vasiṣṭha) becomes a *brahmā*, i.e. "a Bṛhaspati" (ŚB XII.6.1.38-41). ṚV VII.33.14 *yuddhyata* addressed to Indra and his "Bulls" (Maruts) corresponds to BG II.18 *yuddhyasva* addressed to Arjuna. In ṚV V.48.5 Varuṇa "ending the fair garment and operative with his tongue" (*jihváyā . . . ṛñjate cāru vásānaḥ*), i.e. Varuṇa proceeding as Agni the priest "with his purifying ladle" (*pāvakáyā juhvà*, ṚV VI.11.2), is already, like the iconographic Brahmā, "four-faced" (*cáturanīkaḥ*), Agni, the *brahmā* of ṚV IV.9.4 and VII.7.5, himself explicitly "four-sighted" (*caturakṣáḥ*) in ṚV I.31.13, which is rightly understood by Sāyaṇa to mean "facing towards the four directions". (Hermias on *Phaedrus*, "He of the fourfold eyes facing this way, that way".)

The Pāṇḍavas incarnate deities. Arjuna, wearer of the crown or diadem is *kirīṭin* and Draupadī is *Śrī*. Also, bearing in mind that "Arjuna" is Indra (VS X.21, ŚB II.1.2.12 and V.4.3.7), or, what amounts to the same thing, Indra's son (Mbh Parva — ch. 199), that Kṛṣṇa and Arjuna, like Indrāgnī (ṚV VI.59.5) and like Mātali (= Vāyu-Mātariśvan) and Indra (Mbh), share a common car (*purā rājabhyaḥ purohitā eva rathān saṃgṛhṇanty aupadraṣṭyāya nedayam pāpam karavad*), and that "where these are, Kṛṣṇa the Lord of Yoga and Arjuna the Archer, there are fortune, victory, security of being and governmental-science" (*nīti*, BG XVIII.78) — it is clear that

Kṛṣṇa is the Sacerdotium (*brahma*), as is Arjuna the Regnum (*kṣatra*), and Kṛṣṇa therefore to be equated with the Agni–Bṛhaspati–Vasiṣṭha, *brahma*, etc. of ṚV. It is just because Arjuna is Indra — that Indra who is *idaṁ-dra* because he alone saw Brahma (AA II.4 = Ait. Up. I.1, similarly JB III.203, cf. JUB IV.20-21 = Kena Up. 14f.) — that he alone is able to see Kṛṣṇa's "supreme form" (BG XI.47-48). The BG is an Arthaśāstra; its burden of the control of the senses and conquest of self is identical with that which Kauṭilya describes as "the whole of this science" of government.

Why then is Kṛṣṇa "black", as the name implies, or "blue-black", and Arjuna, as again the name implies, "white"? In the first place, the "drop" that in ṚV VIII.96.13-15 takes birth (*avatiṣṭhati,* the regular expression used of the *ātman* when it mounts the bodily vehicle) as Indra's fellow, and for which he has been longing, is "Black" (*kṛṣṇa*): according to Sāyaṇa, this "Kṛṣṇa" is the name of an *asura*, presumably "Viśvarūpa, the son of Tvaṣṭṛ, a sister's son of the *asuras*, who was the *purohita* of the gods" (TS II.5.1.1), i.e. Bṛhaspati, *asurya* son of Tvaṣṭṛ, ṚV II.23.2 and 17, and/or that "Uśanas *kāvya* of the *asuras*" (TS II.5.8.5) with whom Kṛṣṇa identifies himself in BG X.37. Again because Agni and Indra are respectively the Golden Person in the Sun (Death in ŚB X.5.2.13) and the bright Sun itself (ŚB X.4.1.5), as in the eye, where the black (*kṛṣṇa*) represents Agni and the white (*śukla*) Indra (BU II.2.2); "the blue, the deep black" (*nīlam paraḥ kṛṣṇam*), i.e. the pupil, of the solar and the microcosmic eyes corresponding to the masculine, spiritual power (*ama,* Agni, Vāyu, Āditya, *ātman, sāman,* etc.) and "the shining white" (*śuklam bhās*) to the feminine temporal dominion (*sā,* Earth, Air, Sky, vision, *ṛc,* etc.), CU I.6 and 7. Cf. TS III.1.1 "dark colour (*nīlī*) and his beauty do not leave him", when *nīla* is the proper colour of the initiate, who would by no means turn pale. It is clear that Kṛṣṇa's *asurya varṇa* is that of the Divine Darkness, and does not imply a local origin from any swarthy aboriginal people, except in the ontological sense that the *asuras* are "aborigines".

6. The reference is to the performance of the sacrifice, which is the primary "work" of the king above (Indra as Viśvakarmā, ṚV VIII.98.2) as it is of earthly kings. Inasmuch as the king is the executive (*kartṛ*), his is essentially the *karma-mārga,* the "active life", as distinguished from the *jñāna-mārga,* the "contemplative life", of the brāhmaṇa. Further, it will be seen that in giving Agni his "due"

or "share" (*bhāga*) — from Agni's point of view *namasyantaś ca mām bhaktyā,* as in BG IX.I4 — Indra becomes a *bhaktṛ,* just as in ṚV X.51.8-9 where Agni demands his "share of the oblation" (*haviṣo datta bhāgam*) the gods who grant it are *bhaktṛ*s. The like is implied for the human sacrificer who gives his "portion" (*bhāga*) to Agni (ṚV II.10.6) and "in appointing to each their share, endears the gods" (*yathā bhāgam tad devatāḥ prīṇāti,* AB III.4 and 38); cf. ŚB I.9.3.8 for *bhakti* as a share in the sacrifice to the gods, and ṚV IV.2.8, 10, where the generous sacrificer "in offering the oblation, endeareth Thee" (*priyaṁ vā tvā kṛṇavate haviṣmān*) and ib. 14 where "dear to Thee be his invocation". So also in TS V.4.5.4 where Agni "endeared by the gift of his own portion (*svena bhāgadheyena prītaḥ*), burns away the sacrificer's evil" (*pāpmānam api dahati*); cf. TS II.1.4.6 where Indra approaches Agni "with his own share" and Agni then burns away the sixteen coils of Vṛtra in which Indra is wrapped, and in like manner in the case of "whoever approaches him with his own share (*svena bhāgadheyenopasṛtaḥ*), Agni burns up his evil", and "approaches" might have been rendered by "takes refuge with"; the preceding texts from TS are echoed in BU VI.3.1 *bhāgadheyaṁ juhomi,* etc., and the gods having been thus "delighted" (*tṛptāh*), "may they delight me" (*mā . . . tarpayntu*, and a reciprocity is implied as much as it is in the older *bhakti* texts; it is never for nothing that a man devotes himself. The "sacrificial offering" (*yajñiyam bhāgam*) to which Agni moves in ṚV X.124.3, in the same way implies a *bhaktṛ,* here again doubtless Indra. That "Thou art ours and we are thine" (ṚV VIII.92.32) implies no less a mutual loyalty. Like that of thane and earl or wife and husband (cf. the oaths in AB VIII.15), that belongs to the very essence of '*bhakti*'.

The *bhakti* "tone" of ṚV V.46.1 (*kayo na vidvān ayuji svayam. . . nāsyā. . . vaśmi*, etc., corresponding to I.190.4 *atyo na yaṅsad yakṣabhṛd vicetāḥ*) and that of VII.86.7 (*araṁ dāso na mīḷahuṣe karāṇy aham*) as in BG IX.14-15 is unmistakable. The sacrificer is identified with the oblation (*havir vai dīkṣitaḥ,* TS VI.1.4.5); it is himself that he devotes (ŚB *passim*); the sacrifice is a symbolic suicide (*ātmānam ālabhate,* AB 11.3; cf. Eggeling's note on ŚB I.2.3.5 and the designation of the sacrificer as *ātmayājī* in Maitri Up. VI.10). AB III.8 combines the notions of the contemplation (*dhyāna*) of a deity, the offering of an oblation and that of sacrifice with an "endearment" (*yasyai devatāyai havir gṛhītām syāt tāṁ dhyāyed . . . sākṣād eva tad devatām prīṇāti, pratyakṣād devatām yajati*), and AB III.20 *yathā bhāgam devatāḥ priṇāti.* There is no real difference between the implications of these Vedic and Brāhmaṇa texts and that of, for example, BG XII.19 "He that hath devotion is dear to me" (*bhaktimān me priyo naraḥ*). It would be naïve to maintain that the Vedic sacrificer, who certainly performed "devotions" was not also "devoted", or that he never loved the "Friend" (Mitra).

7. Note the singular. The Mixta Persona of Mitrāvaruṇau, Supreme Identity of Conjoint Principles, is the same as that of the "One *akṣara* that is both Agni the Sacerdotium and Indra the Regnum" (ŚB X.4.1.9); cf. ṚV I.108.7 "Whether ye, Indrāgnī, take your pleasure at home (*sve duroṇé*, i.e. *guhyam, ab intra*) or in the Sacerdotium and the Regnum" *brahmáṇi rājani vā*, i.e. *prādur, ab extra*, in active administration). With *sve duroṇé* here cf. JB I.146 *yathāgṛham . . . yathājñāti, vā*, and KU II.25. The Vedic "dual" divinities imply, for the most part at least, a biunity (syzygy) of conjoint principles, active and passive in mutual relationship or both active in relation to things externally administered. The names of such dual divinities cannot always be adequately rendered by the simple use of an adjunctive particle. The resources of language and iconography are inadequate to the representation of an identity of contraries, such as *chāyātapau* or *yin* and *yang:* we cannot think of contraries as coincident, but only as associated, and it may be, reconciled; in other words, the truth of this truth (*satyasya satyam*) is paradoxical, *satyena channam.* Thus Mitrāvaruṇau *is* not an aggregate or mere composition of an essence and a nature, but the one Mixta Persona of both: while at the same time they *are* Mitra and Varuṇa, and whatever is born of such a pair proceeds *ex principio conjunctivo.* The *dvaitībhāva* of MU VII.II is by no means a contradiction of *advaita,* for just as in Christian doctrine, essence and nature, being and existence, mercy and majesty are one in God. (cf. Philo. *Sac.* 59 — God's majesty and goodness, himself *sis ōg's mesos tripas*). Monophysitism would have been as much a heresy from the Indian as from the Christian point of view.

The priority of the counsel (*kratu*) to the power (*dakṣa*), i.e. of the contemplative to the active life, is already explicit in ṚV VIII.13.1 where Indra purifies the former and so gains the latter.

It should be here noted that the order in which the component parts of a dual appear is purely grammatical (cf. Caland on PB VII.6.9, and Pāṇini II.2.34 where *śūdrāryau* means "an ārya and a śūdra"): the form Indrāgnī, for example, if taken literally to be

"Indra and Agni" would be ineffective, it is "Agni and Indra" (ṚV III.25.4) that is to be understood, for as AB II.37 remarks, "These two as Indrāgnī were not victorious, but as Agnendrau they won".

"Regarded as paramount Lord, Agni is Indra") *indraḥ paramaiśvaryo 'gniḥ,* Sāyaṇa on ṚV V.2.3.); "Agni is Indra to the mortal worshipper" (ṚV V.3.1 and ŚB XIV.2.2.42 "Agni, the greatest of Indras").

8. Literally, "these two are of himself", i.e. "these are his two natures". "For we must distinguish two things, the will and the power" (St. Augustine, *De spir. et lit.*, 53). "Two powers are first distinguished (*schizontai*) from the Logos, a poetic (*kāvya*), according to which the artist ordains all things and which is called God (= brahma); and the royal power (= *kṣatra*) of him called the Lord (= *īśvara*) by which he controls all things" (Philo as cited by Brehier, *Les idées . . . de philon d'Alexandre,* 1925, pp. 113-14). "God was not Lord until he had a creature subject to himself" (St. Thomas Aquinas, *Sum. Theol.*, I, 13.7. *ad* 6).

The "two selves " are the "two forms" of Brahma (BU II.3, etc.), the "dual nature" (*dvaitībhāva*) of the "Great Self" (*mahātman*) in accordance with which he participates in both the "true" and the "false" (*satyānṛtopabhogārthaḥ,* MU VII.11.8), or, as this might have been otherwise expressed, in virtue of which he is the common source of *deva*s and *asura*s, that is, participates both in divine and human experience, the gods being the truth and men untruth (ŚB III.9.4.1). The trace of the divine biunity appears in the two selves of the man who is *dvyātman* (JB I.17, etc., see n. 84).

Thus the *purohita* is "the half of the self of the kṣatriya" (*ardhātmo ha vā eṣa kṣatriyasya,* AB VII.26), as are Sky and Earth (AA III.1.2) and as is the man of the woman (ŚB X.5.2.8, and BU I.4.4), and neither is complete without the other (ŚB VIII.6.1.12, V.2.1.10 and XIV.1.3.25), as also holds for Kṛṣṇa and Arjuna (Mbh II.20.3 and 14). Hence the use of *sārdham,* literally "plus a half", in connection with any complementary union, as in JUB I.48.7 where Prajāpati *sārdhaṁ samait,* i.e. "coupled with" Vāc. It is thus literally true that "the *purohita* was in religion and civil affairs the *alter ego* of the king" (ŚB IV.1.4.5-6, AB VIII.24; cf. AB Keith, *Rel. and Phil. of the Veda and Upanishads,* 1925, p. 292), or as we should rather say, the king the *alter ego* of the *purohita*. For this does not mean that the two "halves" are reciprocally equal; on the contrary, the relation of one to the other is that of part to whole (cf. AA III.I.I where *manas* and *vāc* are two halves with *satyam* their *sandhi*). The "only Vrātya" (*Brahmā, brahma, prāṇa, Vāmana*, KU V.3) is the source of the *brahma* and the *kṣatra* (AV X.2.22, 23 and 10.3 — as rightly understood by Aufrecht, *pace* Whitney — where *brahma* is the origin of *kṣatra;* so also ŚB XII.7.3.12), the *brahma* (Brahmā) is both the *brahma* and the *kṣatra* (ŚB X.4.1.9 and TS III.5.7 where *Parṇa* = *brahma* and *brahma+kṣatra*), Agni is both Mitra and Varuṇa (R̥V VIII.12.3; ŚB VI.6.3.5; VI.7.4.6 Agni = Indrāgni, IX.4.1.16 "this Agni is both the priesthood and the nobility"). In the case of Manas and Vāc, Vāc is the lesser, "for Manas is by far the more unlimited (*aparimitataram*) and Vāc by far the more limited" (*parimitatarā*, ŚB I.4.4.7, cf. I.4.5.11), and these are the two aspects of Prajāpati, who is "both the limited and unlimited" (*parimitāparinita,* ŚB VII.2.2.14, etc.) The infinite, in other words, always includes the finite as "its own", of which it cannot be deprived, whether logically or really (cf. AV X.8.29 and BU V.l): It is the finite nature that can be logically, if not really, isolated from the infinite, and therefore stands in need of a "completion". Cf. R̥V III.31.2 where, of Agni's parents, "one empowers (*r̥ṇdhan*), the other is the agent (*karttā*)".

9. The relation, in other words, is that of patron to artist, or in the artist that of art to operation, *actus primus* to *actus secundus.* And just as the king is only legitimately such to the extent that he does the will of a higher power — "Thy will be done on earth as it is in heaven" — so the *artifex* as an efficient cause is only free to the extent that he agrees with the patron and is governed by his art, or, if not, is merely a "worker", a "hand", compelled by economic pressure or driven by his own sweet will or fancy.

10. *Agre:* not *ante principium* (where there is only the Supreme Identity, *tad ékam, yáthā strīpúmāṅsau sampāriṣvaktau,* BU I.4.3), but with reference to the separation of the male and female principles, sky and earth, etc., in *principio,* because of which they are alien to one another until reunited by marriage: *āgre* here and *sr̥ṣṭaū* in ŚB X.4.1.5 imply "before the reign begins" or "at the beginning of the reign" (*pūrvakāle yasya rāṣṭrasya,* Sāyaṇa on AB VIII.I and as in PB VII.6.10); *sr̥ṣṭaṁ nānā* in ŚB X.4.1.5 corresponding to "twofold in the beginning" (*dvayám . . . ágre*).

    Agre corresponds to *in principio* (Gen. I.1), now rendered "in the beginning", but which almost all mediaeval commentators, from

St. Augustine (*Conf.* XII.20, 27, 29) onwards, have understood to mean "in the first principle", *in verbo, in sapientia,* etc., without reference to time.

11. *Ṛté* implies not only a spatial separation, but an opposition.
12. Cf. D.11.259 *purakkhatvā* (*puraskṛ*) = "serving".
13. ŚB II.6.3.8 — "Sūrya governs all this (world), now by means of a good, now by a bad king"; and *Par.* XIII.108 — "Kings, which are many, and the good ones few".
14. The root in *sūya, sava, sūta,* etc., is *sū*. Many scholars distinguish two roots *sū,* (1) to "impel" or "instigate" and (2) to "quicken" or "generate". The latter meaning is obvious im ṚV VIII.101.3 where *sūte* (begets) is opposed to *staríḥ* (sterile). In I.146.5 where Agni, the "Sun of Men" is *sūḥ,* i.e. *prasavitā, utpādayitā* (Sāyaṇa) in relation to all things, in ṚV I.113. where *savituḥ savā́ya* is "for the birth of Savitṛ" himself, and in BU VI.4.19 where Savitṛ, "He of true quickening" (*satyáprasava*), is invoked in the marriage rite, certainly as progenitive deity, Gandharva and Divine Eros. In our contexts it is this Savitṛ that is the primary instigator or quickener (MU VI.7 *savanāt savitā*). If in some contexts *sū* is rather to "instigate" than to "quicken" (cf. *sūyate = anujña yate,* AV IV.8.1. Comm.), and may be replaced by forms of *iṣ* or causative forms of *ṛ* (as in AB II.5), this is because it is only when Manas and Vāc are "personified" (as is usual in our texts, Manas being identified with Prajāpati, and Vāc as his daughter) that we realize that the consequence of an "instigation" of Vāc by Manas (or the *brahma*) is an embodiment of what has been "conceived" and is a "concept" (BU II.2.3): the intellectual principle inseminating the mother of which it is to be born, just as in any other aspect of a Logos doctrine. To "instigate" or "set in motion" or "move" is thus only a weaker value of "quicken": the *purohita* is really "fathering" his "counsel" on the king who as the *kartṛ* is to give it effect by means of his *fiat.* And this is only an extension of the acts of aspersion, etc., by which the king has already been "begotten" (*sūtáḥ*) and "brought to birth" (*prásūtaḥ*) — for this distinction cf. KB V.3 *prajā. . . sṛṣṭā aprasūtaḥ = Avyakta Up.* VI.I. *prajāḥ sṛṣṭvā na jāyante,* and BU I.4.11 where the *kṣatra* is *sṛṣtam,* but evidently *aprasūtam* until the Rājasūya has taken place.

Eggeling discusses his translation of *sū* in *SBE* XLI, p. 2, n. 1. We adopt his usual rendering, "quicken". His occasional use of "spiriter", although true to the essential values, since here as in

John VI.63 *spiritus est qui vivificat,* is too awkward to be adopted. We have no doubt that the "two" roots *sū* are, or were originally, one.

The octad of king-making deities (Savitṛ, Agni, Bṛhaspati, Indra, Rudra, Mitra and Varuṇa) who endow the king with a variety of powers or virtures correspond to the "good fairies" of folklore who bring their gifts to the newly-born solar hero.

15. Buddhas asperse (*abhisic*) *bodhisattvas* with their own hands.

16. The word *abhiṣeka* is too often, and especially by translators from the Pāli, rendered by "Coronation". It is true that Indra wears a crown and is *kirīṭin* accordingly, that Rudra is turbaned (*uṣṇiṣin*) and that the Mahāpurīṣa is *uṇhisosīso,* but the putting on of crown or turban plays no important part in the early Indian rites, where it is an "Aspersion" rather than a "Coronation" that makes the king.

    not all the water in the rough rude sea
    can wash the balm from an anointed king.

17. For the priest as the sacrificer's "father in God" see *JAOS* 60, 1940, pp. 50-51. It must be understood that the Rājasūya is "a congruous rite" (*tat saloma kriyate,* ŚB V.3.5.26), so that all that is said elsewhere of the ritual death and rebirth of the sacrificer can be applied to the king, *a fortiori.* Accordingly, "He who performs the Rājasūya becomes the "child of the waters. . . . He (the priest) brings him to birth" (*janayati,* "delivers", in the medical sense and analogically). ŚB V.3.5.19-24 — a generation that corresponds to that of Indra as king in ṚV VIII.97.10 *tatakṣur indraṁ jajanuṣ ca rājase,* comparable to X.61.7 *ajanayan brahma devā vāstospatiṁ vratapāṁ niratakṣan,* and X.66.I3 *kṣetrasya patim.* And this is why the Rājasūya is also the Varuṇasava, for the ritual employs the text of VS X.7 where Varuṇa enthroned in the dwellings of men, is called the "Child of the Water". If this is more often an epithet of Agni, it is in place here because the nascent Agni "is Varuṇa" and "becomes Mitra" only when "kindled" (ṚV V.3.1), and the sacrificer's regeneration is likewise a "kindling" (ŚB IV.4.5.23). The intention is to enthrone as king, not a "Varuṇa", but a "Mitra".

    As Hocart has remarked with reference to rites of royal installation, "The theory is that the king (1) dies, (2) is reborn, (3) as a god" (*Kingship,* 1927, p. 70). In this sequence, however, he was unable to recognize the "death" in the Indian sources, chiefly ŚB, although he recognized that all regeneration necessarily implies an antecedent death. As to this, it must be remembered that any initiatory rebirth, or indeed a birth of any kind, implies a previous death; for initiatory death may be cited JUB III.9.4 *enam etad dīkṣayanti . . . mṛtasya vāvaiṣa tadā rūpam bhavati.* Any sacrifice is a symbolic suicide; it is himself that the sacrificer to the gods, to Agni (AB II.3 *ātmānam ālabhate,* and ŚB *passim*); cf. my "Ātmayajña" in *HJAS* VI.358-98 (1942). Moreover, the installation of a king parallels not only that of Varuṇa, but that of King Soma, and although it is for a "supreme sovereignty" and "not for slaying thee" that Soma is bought, nevertheless "when they press him they slay him" (ŚB III.3.2.8), saying: "Fear not . . . it is the evil that is slain, not Soma" and "Thereby he slays all his evil (*sarvaṁ pāpmānaṁ hanti,* VS VI.35 and ŚB III.9.4.17-18). The beating of the king which puts him above the law, so that he can do no wrong (ŚB V.4.4.7) is analogous to the pressing of Soma by which "his evil" is removed (TS VI.4.8 slaughter of Soma). In the same way the expiatory bath with which a sacrifice concludes, taken not in flowing (living) but in Varuṇya (stagnant) waters, is a kind of death (cf. CU III.17.5 *manaṇam evāvabhṛthaḥ*), and comparable in this respect to a baptism; the immersion is for the sake of a liberation from all that pertains to Varuṇa, i.e. from evil, and by it "just as a serpent casts its skin, so is the sacrificer freed from all evil (*sárvasmāt pāpmáno nirmucyate*), there does not remain in him even so much sin (*énas*) as there is in a child" (*yávat kumāre,* ŚB IV.4.5.23), words which, applied to a king, would mean "even so much evil as there was in him when a prince". Thus in various ways the king "dies" and is reborn; the old, Vāruṇya, man is put off, and the new, Maitreya, man put on, a change that is reflected in the investiture with new garments which follows the immersion, cf. AV XIV.2.44 "Clothing myself anew . . . as a bird from an egg, I am freed from all sin".

Such an absolution is essential. The king is, indeed, "another man" in the sense of I Sam. X.6. Hocart cites the fourteenth-century Jean Golein who held "that the king is as much cleansed of his sins" as one takes orders (*Kingship,* p. 93). Charles I wore white robes at his Coronation "to declare that Virgin purity with which he came to be espoused unto his kingdom" (Heylin, *Cyprianus Anglicus,* 1668, p. 145), "Espoused to his kingdom", i.e. as *bhūpati,* "Husband of the earth": for just as the king is the "wife" of the priest, so is the earth in turn *his* "wife": just as Soma is united to "these quarters of space as his bride (*ābhir digbhir mithunéna*), with his dear domain" (*priyéṇa dhámnā*, ŚB III.9.4.20), so is the human king to his own land (*deśa*), the shooting of arrows to the four quarters in the *digvijaya* rite being evidently a symbolic demonstration of this relationship. The quarters are, of course, always feminine in relation to their centre and meeting point; e.g. R̥V IX.113.2 where Soma is *diśām pati*, cf. AV II.10.4, AA II.2.3, ŚB III.9.4.21.

18. "Apart from a coincidence of these two, political power and philosophy, there can be no cessation of evils, whether for the state or for the individual" (*Republic* 473 D; also E.R. Goodenough, *Philo*, p. 190; see n. 57, p. 109).

19. BU IV.1.6 *mano vai samrāṭ paramaṁ brahma*; *manas* in all our texts and as identified with Prajāpati, *passim*, is the scholastic *intellectus vel spiritus* (intellect as well as spirit) the divine mind and will, and it is only later that *manas* in the sense of external mind or reason and modern "intellect" is subordinated to *buddhi* as "pure intellect"; our *manas* in other words is *nous*, as in Hermes I.6, 11b where "The Father is *nous*, the Mother *physis*, *logos* the Son". *Manas*, for ŚB X.5.3.1, is that Supreme Identity (*tadekam*) that was in the beginning when "this" universe neither was nor was not (R̥V X.129.1-2). As remarked by Keith, *manas* in the narrower sense of mental "organ" appears first in Kauṣ. Up. III (AA, p. 46); this lower and merely rational "mind" is the seat of "opinion" rather than of knowledge (MU VI.30). The "two minds", pure and impure, are distinguished in MU VI.34.6 and elsewhere, as in Plato and Philo. The word *metanoein*, "to change one's mind" implies the replacement of the impure by the pure *nous*.

20. Cf. Aeschylus, *Suppl.* 595f. παρεστι δ ἔργον ως ἔπος *paresti d'ergon hōs epios* (*epos*).

21. Cf. Morel *Egyptian Civilization*, p. 377.

22. That it is the king's function by his fiat to give expression to the spiritual counsel, implies the traditional doctrine that human law echoes or reflects Divine Law. Thus, for example, the king, "who was to be a 'divine man' and so link the people with the spiritual order" is regarded as "the incarnate representation of supreme and universal Law. In him that Law, itself unformulated, could become vocal (λογικός, *logikos*); that is, the ideal man had the power of taking a law which was spirit and divine purpose, and of applying

it to human problems. Through him the Law, or nature of God, could become statutory laws, and true laws for society could never, it was universally believed, be had in any other way" (Goodenough, *An Introduction to Philo Judacus*, 1940, pp. 38-39).

23. Also ŚB IV.6.7.5-6. Nothing is *done* unless Vāc voices commands of mind, "Do this". Mind alone does not *act*. Cf. MU III.2 and Hermes XII.1.2, 4.11 and XII.1.13A, from which *vāc, phone* is distinct from *logos*.

24. On unregulated speech, see Philo, *De Somniis* II.260.

25. Comparable to Śaṅkara's commentary on BU I.4.14, *satyam iti yathā śāstrārthatā sa evānuṣṭhīyamānô dharmanāmā bhavati* ["Truth" is the fact of being in accordance with the scriptures. The same thing, when it is practised, is called righteousness. . . .]

26. Just as in ŚB IV. 1.4.3 "whatever the Regnum does (*yad dha kiṁ ca . . . karma cakré*) unquickened (*aprasūtam*) by the sacerdotium, therein it fails (*na . . . samānṛdhe*) or conversely "succeeds" (*ānṛdhe*). We see from this collation that *kṛta* and *saṁṛddha, akṛta* and *asaṁṛddha* are equivalents: that what is "misdone" is really "not done" at all.

See Plato *Sophist* 237; falsehood is what is "unsaid" and misfeasance is non-feasance. Cf. Skr. *abhūtavādī*, a liar, and Ger. Unthat corresponds to "nothing". Finally Manu VIII.127 *kautasākṣyam kṛtam . . . cāpyakṛtam bhavet* (= "whatever has been done must be [considered as] undone"); BU I.4.15 *akṛtam*. Thus the privative *a* in *akṛta* does not deny an event, but asserts that the event was not an act but a failure to "act". The verb "to act" has strictly speaking only a good and positive sense, as when we speak of God as "all in act"; a sin is not an "act" but an "omission".

In TS VI.4.9.5, full vessels represent things done in the sacrifice, as contrasted with things "not done"; only acts and not omissions, repel the *rākṣasas*. St. Thomas Aquinas in the same way speaks of the sinner as "non-existent" (*Sum. Theol.*, I.20.2 ad 4), not meaning to say that no one sins. In the same way, too, *asat*, literally "not being", is also in many contexts "naught-y", i.e. evil; not a mere nothingness, but a mere potentiality. All these propositions depend on the principle *ens et bonum convertuntur* (= being and goodness meet), common to all traditional metaphysics. In BG XVII.27-28 *sat* and *asat* are in all cases categories of what the Nominalist would call "real" things. In JUB I.53.1 the two worlds — sky and earth, with all their equivalents, mas. and fem. — are respectively *sat* and *asat.*

The question is of importance in connection with the so-called Vedāntic doctrine of "illusion". It is evident that whatever is an "appearance" (*rūpa*) must be an appearance of something and that whatever "significance" (*nāman*) is attached to this appearance must involve a correct or an incorrect interpretation of its basis. It is by means of the intelligible and the sensible, "name and appearance" (*nāma rūpa*), that which is referred to by Vāc and recognized by Manas, that Brahmā, *Deus absconditus* (*bráhmaivá parārdhám agacchat*), "returned (*pratyávait*, "came down again", i.e. descended as *avatāra*) to these worlds which are coextensive with what can be sensed and named" (ŚB XI.2.3.3-6, cf. BU I.4.7, S. II.101, D II.63, 64), becoming thus, and thus "enjoying", both what is "real" (*satya*) and what is "false" (*anṛta*, TU II.6, cf. MU VII.28.8); it is, indeed, by a marriage of these two, *satya* and *anṛta*, affirmation (*oṁ*) and negation (*na*), that man is propagated and multiplied (*tayor mithunāt prajāyate bhūyān bhavati*, AA II.3.6). Our functional existence, unlike our being, is logical and analytical, determined equally by what we are not and what we are; we distinguish subject from object and content from form.

There are, of course, "true" and "false" names of things; the former correspond to their essences or formative ideas and the latter to our own thinking, ŚB XI.3.2.5, having in mind the latter and conventional nomenclature, remarks that of these two, "name and appearance", the latter is the "greater". From this point of view it is the appearance that is "real" and the name that is "false"; it is not our senses but our interpretations that are at fault; we *do see* the glitter (cf. BU V.14.4), bat are wrong in assuming that all that glitters is gold (Arist. *Met.* IV.6.23). An ascription of "unreality" to temporalia does not mean that appearances to not appear, but that we are mistaken in describing them as "things" and not simply as appearances, and misguided in trying to find out what they are instead of asking "of what" are they the appearances (cf. ŚA VS = Kauṣ U. III.8); mistaken in assuming that these are the appearances of any thing, rather than of a protean no-thing "veiled in all things" (BU II.5.18). It is remarkable that in discussing this very question of the world Sextus Empiricus makes use of the familiar Indian parable of the snake and the rope (ŚB IV.4.5.3 "snakes are like rope"), saying that the sceptics by no means "abolish phenomena" but only "question whether the underlying object is such as it appears. . . . our doubt does not concern the appearance itself but the account given of the appearance" (*Pyrrhonism* I.227-28). St. John Chrysostom, *Homilies on the Gospels,* of Matthew 6.23; "Just as men in the dark see nothing clearly, taking a rope for a serpent . . . so rich men shrink from what is in no way terrible for one who has eyes". So also Heracleitus (*Aph.* IV and XII taken together). This is precisely the Vedantic position: the rope is not a snake, nor even "really" a rope, but "really" a manifestation of Brahma, "the Real who becomes whatever there is here" (TU II.6 and Arist. *Met.* IV.5.23 "And as concerning truth, that not every appearance is 'true', we shall say first"). In the same way, as we have repeatedly pointed out, *māyā* does not mean an "illusion" as distinct from a real phenomenon, but rather the means of creating any appearance whatever: that these worlds are *māyāmaya* does not mean that they do not "exist", but that they are quantitative, or "material" in the sense of the etymologically equivalent *mātrā*, "measure", to be understood in the sense of Heracleitus XX, "ever-living fire, in measures (*metra*) being kindled and in measures going out" (*aposbennumenon = nirvāta,* as applicable to fire, wind and passion); to these "measures" of Heracleitus (cf. Plato, *Timaeus* 45 BCE where vision is a part of the internal fire) correspond the *tejomātrāḥ* of BU IV.4.1 = *prāṇāgnayaḥ* of Praśna Up. IV.3, i.e. the human elementals or "powers of the soul".

For *māyā,* from √*mā* and as denoting the principle of measurement and thus the means of creation see "Nirmāṇakāya" in *JRAS* 1938, pp. 81-84, and AV XIII.2.3 and 5, *nānārūpe ahanī karṣi māyayā . . . divaṁ ca sūrya pṛthivīṁ ca devīm ahorātre vimimāno yad éṣi.*

27. "We cannot speak or name correctly by speaking as we like but only by speaking in accordance with the ascertained nature of the things referred to" — Plato, *Cratylus* 387.

28. ŚB XIII.1.5.1-6 Concert of two Brāhmanical lute players — one should be a brāhmaṇa and the other a rājanya, corresponding to *brahma+kṣatra.*

29. "This righteousness is the controller of the kṣatriya. Therefore there is nothing higher than that". — BU I.4.14, Śvet. Up. I.12.

30. "Became of one form" suggests the important problem, to what extent the Rājasūya endows the king with a priestly character, as in the Roman Imperial Rite in which the Emperor kneels before the

Pope, who *facit eum dericum* (makes as a cleric) and mitres as well as crowns him (R.M. Wooley, *Coronation Rites*, 1915, p. 50). The problem is not an easy one, but certainly the statement by Keith that "the connection of royalty with priestly rank, if it had ever been a motif of the growth of the kingship (in India), had long disappeared before the time of the Saṁhitās" (*Veda of the Black Yajus School*, cxii-cxiii), is far too sweeping. ŚB V.1.1.12-13 "Unfit for kingship is the brāhmaṇa (*na vai brāhmaṇo rājyāyālam*). . . . Rājasūya for the king, Vājapeya for the brāhmaṇa; former bestows kingship, latter empire". (Nevertheless kings do perform Vājapeya). Kingship is not enough for the brāhmaṇa, who would not desire it. It must be borne in mind, again, that the Rājasūya is an "analogous" rite, and that every sacrificer, being reborn of the sacrifice, the Spiritual power (*brahma*), is born a brahmāṇa (*brāhmaṇa* patronymic from *brahma*), and the initiate (*dīkṣita*) is for this reason to be addressed as a brāhmaṇa, whatever his caste may have been (ŚB III.2.1.40): "the sacrifice is the Sacerdotium (*brahma*), the initiate is born again of the sacrifice . . . he attains to priesthood" (*brāhmaṇatām upaiti*, AB VII.22-3, PB V.3.10).

ŚB I.1.4.6 "For the priest (*brāhmaṇa*) is the repeller of the *rākṣasas* . . .", with Eggeling's note — "Only a brāhmaṇa can perform sacrifice. If, as is permitted in certain ceremonies, a kṣatriya or vaiśya officiates, he, as it were, becomes a brāhmaṇa (and is addressed as such) for the occasion, by means of the *dīkṣā*, or rite of initiation."

It is certain that Indra, the archetypal king, functions also as priest (*brahmā*, ṚV VIII.16.7, ŚB IV.6.6.5) and as Cantor (*udgātṛ*, JUB I.22.2), a prophet (*ṛṣi*, ṚV VIII.6.4) and that he is constantly identified with the Sun. King Keśin (the Keśin Dārbhya of JB II.53-54; JUB III.29, and KB VII.4; cf. ṚV X.136) functions as the *gṛhapati* of a *sattra* (ŚB XI.8.4.1). On the sacrificer as *gṛhapati* of a *sattra*, see ŚB IV.6.8.3-5. Weber thought this a survival from a former age (*Indische Studien*, X.25.94), but this is not acceptable, since whereas *formerly* only Vāsiṣṭhas could function as the *brahmā* TS III.5.2.1, ŚB IV.6.6.5), *now* anyone having the requisite knowledge can be a Brāhmaṇa and may be addressed as Brahmā (ŚB IV.6.6.5, XII.6.1.10), the Brāhmaṇas and Upaniṣads thus anticipating the supposedly Buddhist distinction of the "Brāhmaṇa by birth" (*brahma-bandhu*, CU VI.1.1) from the Brāhmaṇa by knowledge, Brāhmaṇa as *brahmavit*. We learn, too, that "formerly, an inveterated king aspersed his own son" (Comm.

on ŚB XIII.8.3.19 where "the kṣatriya asperses the kṣatriya", cf. Mbh I.69.44, Poona edn., where Duṣyanta *bharatam . . . yauvarājye 'bhyaṣecayat*), a practice that seems to have survived in Siam in connection with the very important rite of the tonsure of the heir-apparent in which the king, impersonating Śiva, "poured the contents of the great chank shell upon the head of the prince" (H.G. Quaritch Wales, *Siamese State Ceremonies*, 1931, p. 130), cf. AB VIII.13 where Indra is anointed by Prajāpati, and LS, p. 100 where *buddhas* asperse (*abhisic*) *bodhisattvas* with their own hands.

In the *Mahā-Govinda-sutta* the king himself asperses the *purohita* (D. II.232); and it was probably by an aspersion that the king exercised his own powers of "quickening" (*sava*), when he bestowed accession honours on the eleven members of his court (*senānī, purohita, mahiṣī,* etc.) who are called the "Recipients of Decorations" (*ratninaḥ*, ŚB V.3.1.12 — not to be confused with the "Seven Jewels", *sapta ratnā*, of a Cakravartin, ṚV V.1.5, VI.74.1, BD V.123, although the categories partly coincide). Hocart points out that the "quickening" of the *ratnins* is a ritual deification: it will be observed that excepting the queen there are ten male *ratnins*, and these with the king himself are presumably the "eleven gods on earth" of ṚV I.139.11.

Furthermore, in the Act of Homage, the king is addressed as Brahmā and identified with Savitṛ, Indra, Mitra and Varuṇa, i.e. priestly as well as royal deities, the Brahman taking a seat below him (TS III.5.2.1, ŚB IV.6.6.5, BU I.4.11): while according to Manu (VII.2f.) a kṣatriya who has duly received the "sacerdotal sacrament" (*brāhmam . . . saṁskāram*), i.e. has been initiated and asperged, is a substance compounded in some measure of Indra, Anila (Vāyu), Yama, Arka (Sun), Agni, Varuṇa, Candra (Moon), and Vitteśa (Kubera), and is like the burning sun, so that "no one on earth can look at him who is a great God in human form" (*mahatī devatā . . . nararūpeṇa*). Manu IX.303-12 shows in what way a king exercises analogous functions.

On the other hand, PB XVIII.10.8 expressly reserves the Sacerdotium from the Regnum, and innumerable texts sharply distinguish the Sacerdotal from the Royal functions; it is much rather the Sacerdotium that exercises both (Bṛhaspati as fighting priest, ṚV *passim*), than the Regnum. It is evident that the installation of a king does not dispense with his or the kingdom's need of a priesthood. That the king is the sacrificer (*yajamāna*) and Lord of the Sacrifice (*yajñapati*) does not mean that he normally performs or conducts the rite, but that he is the patron who institutes, pays for and defends the sacrifice on behalf of his people. He is "the supporter of rites" (*dhr̥tavrata*), and as such he may not say or do anything or everything, but only what is correct (*sādhu*); he and the Śrotriya (indoctrinated brāhmaṇa) are the two "supporters of the rite" (*dhr̥távratau*, ŚB V.4.4.5). Indra is typically *vratapā*, "Fidei Defensor"; cf. R̥V X.61.7 where "the effective gods produced the Sacerdotium (*bráhma*), and made the Land's Lord (*vástoṣpátim*), the guardian of the rite (*vratapām*)", cf. R̥V II.13.5, where "generated Indra with lauds and waters" refers to his birth from the sacrifice in the Rājasūya.

The difficulties are best resolved by recalling that the priesthood and the kingship correspond to sky and earth, who were originally one but departed from one another as soon as their unity had been consummated (R̥V *passim*, TS V.1. 5.8, V.2.4.1, BU III.8.9, etc.). In the same way the king is assimilated to and identified with the priest (as Arjuna is sometimes identified with Kr̥ṣṇa in Mbh) for the duration of the nuptial sacrifice, but, just as in any other sacrifice, "becomes again what he really is" when the rite is relinquished, thus returning from divinity to humanity, *satya* to *anr̥ta* (VS I.5 and II.28, ŚB I.1.1.4-6, I.9.3.23, III.6.3.21, III.9.4.1, IX.5.1.12). It is, in fact, explicit, that having put off his Royalty and become a brāhmaṇa, the king in turn abandons this priestly character: "when he concludes, he assume his kṣatriya character, calling to witness Agni, Vāyu, and Āditya (the cosmic *purohitas*) that "Now I am he who I am" (AB VII.22): It is then "not actually and evidently" (*na . . . pratyakṣam*) but only symbolically and in an occult manner (*parokṣam*) that "the kṣatriya assumes the form of the Sacerdotium" (*brahmaṇo rūpam upanigacchati*) and therefore only transubstantially that he can partake of Soma (AB VII.31); cf. JUB I.40.3, where, notwithstanding that the Voice (*vāc*) is the indispensable support of the Sāman, "It is by no means by the voice that the priestly office is performed, but in an occult way" (*parokṣeṇa*), i.e. mentally, in accordance with the injunction *yájadhva. . . . mánasā* R̥V VIII.2.37, cf. TS VI.I.4.5, KB VII.4. In any case, that the king does assume the sacerdotal character, however temporarily and in whatever manner, makes it impossible to say that "the connection of royalty with priestly rank had long disappeared". All we can say is that hardly any trace of any actual exercise of Brāhmanical functions survives in the Brāhmaṇas.

Just as the king assumes a priestly character which he again relinquishes, so "In that he is aspersed (*abhiṣicyate*) in the Rājasūya, he ascends to the world of heaven, (but) if he did not descend again he would either depart thither beyond human beings (i.e. he would die) or would go mad" (PB XVIII.10.10), a condition of equal application to any other sacrificer (TS VII.3.10.3, VII.4. 4.2, AB IV.21, etc.); the ritual deification which, prefigures an effective deification *post mortem* — cf. *Harṣacarita* 215, *devabhūyaṁ gate narendre,* "Now that the king has assumed his Godhead", i.e. has died, and the representation of kings as deties in funerary chapels — would be presently fatal, as is indeed implied by the rule: "No one becomes immortal in the flesh" ŚB X.4.3.9). The royal sacrificer's Himmelfahrt is nevertheless of profound significance: for the descent, a sort of *avataraṇa* comparable to the Buddha's at Saṅkīsa, and to Plato's return of the philosopher to the cave, is "by that stairway which, save to reascend, no one descendeth" (Dante, *Paradiso,* X.86-87). It cannot be wondered at that in D II.227, where Brahmā Sanatkumāra ("The Eternal Youth", i.e. Agni-Bṛhaspati, *devānām brahmā,* cf. AV X.8.44 *ātmanam dhīram ajāraṁ yúvānam*) appears in the Tāvatiṁsa heaven amongst the thirty-three *deva*s beside whom he takes his seat (and with whom he thus "consorts"), each of them experiences a beatitude which is compared to that of "a kṣatriya king whose head has been aspersed (*muddhāvasitto* — aspersion beginning from the head, ŚB IX.4.1.15, etc.) and who as soon as he has been aspersed (*adhunābhisitto*) experiences a sublime enthusiasm and sublime contentment": for the king's relation to his human *brahmā* is precisely that of the several *deva*s to their common Brahmā, cf. n. 4. That the Regnum is only temporarily set above the Sacerdotium in the Act of Homage (TS I.6.16 and ŚB V.4.4.9-13) is also apparent from BU I.4.11, where we are told that the Sacerdotium was one simply in the beginning, and as such did not manifest omnipotence (*vibhu* and *tadekam sanna vyabhavat,* with implication of *vibhava* in the sense of "dominion", cf. n. 41 and *vibhūti* in BG X.40). That (One) manifested a more resplendent form (*śreyo rūpam,* cf. ṚV X.31.2 *śreyāṅsaṁ dakṣam,* "power and glory"), that of the Regnum, even the *deva*s who are dominions (*kṣatrāṇi,* cf. TS II.3.1.4 *vāruṇaṁ vai rāṣṭram*), viz. Indra, Varuṇa, Soma, Rudra, Parjanya, Yama, Mṛtyu,

Īśāna (with some changes of name, this octad is doubtless to be identified with the octad of king-making deities mentioned in n. 14).

There is, accordingly, nothing above the Regnum (BU I.4.11 *kṣatrāt paraṁ nāsti*): in the Rājasūya the brāhmaṇa pays homage to the kṣatriya from a lower position; he expressly glorifies the Regnum (*kṣatra eva tad yaśo dadhāti*). But the Sacerdotium is the source of the Regnum, so that even though a ruling king attains supremacy (*paramatām,* like Varuṇa's in ŚB V.3.3.9), he finally (*antatas,* i.e. when the Rājasūya is ended) leans upon (*upaniśrayati*) the Sacerdotium as his source, and if he (the king) injures him (the brāhmaṇa), he is striking at his own source, and he becomes the worse (*pāpīyān bhavati*), having injured his superior" (*śréyāṅsam*). For *brahma* as the source of *kṣatra,* see AV X.2.22-23 and XV.10.3. Śaṅkara is clearly right in saying that the "glory" and "supremacy" are references to the Act of Homage at the enthronement, but that when the rite is relinquished it is the king who gives precedence" to the *purohita,* whose designation itself purports "Praepositus" (Gr. πρόιτος proitos, *Praeitor*-Spartan Zeùs, 'Αγήτωρ *hagetor,* Agetōr).

Texts, of course, abound, in which the relative inferiority of the king to the priest is affirmed (*rājyam sāmrāj* ŚB V.1.1.12). The brāhmaṇas are not his subjects, "their king is Soma" (the sacrificer has Soma for king, AB I.14, ŚB V.4.2.3, TS 1.8.10d); everything here is "food" for the king, but he himself is "food" for the brāhmaṇas (ŚB V.4.2.3, Sn 619; Kauṣ.Up. II.9); Soma's throne is borne by four men, but the human king's only by two, since Soma rules absolutely all (*asya sakṛt sarvaśreṣṭe*) but not so the other (ŚB III.3.4.26); the brāhmaṇs are not committed to the *kṣatra,* whose "rod" (*daṇḍa*) is not for them, while they on the other hand have a "counter-rod" (*pratidaṇḍa*) that can be used against him or any of his subjects (PB XVIII.10.8), i.e. the power of the curse or excommunication, the case of *Nahuṣa,* who was for a time the king of the gods, providing an example (Hopkins, *Epic Mythology*, p. 130). See *Fug.* 111 — "The kingly diadem, the symbol not of absolute sovereignty but of an admirable viceroyalty"; and "The Bishops are superior in that they consecrate kings, but cannot be consecrated by them" (Letter of Hincmar, Archbishop of Rheims, to Charles the Bald, CE 868).

That the king is inferior in hierarchy to the priest is emphasized by Oldenberg (*Die Religion des Veda,* 1894, pp. 375, 376) and by Weber (*Indische Studien,* X.160 and "Über den Rājasūya". *Königliche*

Akademische Wissenschaft, Phil.-Hist. Köln, 1893, p. 118). See Philostratus III.10.

Oldenberg (p. 376) speaks of the "sacerdotal prestige which far exceeded weakly developed royal individualities", while Weber ("Rājasūya", remarks that "the sharp emphasis on the subordination of the king, which is evident throughout the whole of the *Aitareya Brāhmaṇa*, is absent in the Epics", and refers to the absolute necessity for a king to have a *purohita* (= domestic chaplain) — otherwise the gods will not accept his offerings — and to be submissive and obedient to him". See n. 56 and ŚB XI.4.2.17-18, XI.5.3.9 on *gṛhapati*. Weber's "absent in the Epics" reminds us that the Temporal Power in India, as in Europe, gradually freed itself from its originally legitimate status of agent (*kartṛ*) of the Spiritual Authority, and that as remarked by Rhys Davids in *Dialogues* 2.267, n. 1, with reference to the position of the king as described in the *Mahā-Govinda-Sutta*, "a king was of lower rank then than now". This last is the same as it would be to say that Satan was of lower rank before his fall than after the assertion of his independence. How different from our own are the traditional values of feudalism may be seen in the fact that the slave was once regarded as the superior of the hired man: a colleague of mine, while living in Persia remarked to a messenger, "I suppose you are the Sheikh's servant", and received the proud answer, "No sir, I am his *slave*". We have learnt to confuse servility with loyalty and rebellion with freedom. ("For the slave is a partner in his master's life, but the artisan is more remote". Aristotle, *Pol.* I.5.10). In fact, "Hereditary service (serfdom) is entirely incompatible with modern industrialism, *and that is why it is always painted in such dark colours*" (A.M. Hocart, *Les Castes*, 1938, p. 238, [italics mine], and "We must not be misled by the European equivalents for some Indian words", p. 70).

Vrata is "operation" (*vratam iti karma nāma*, Sāyaṇa on ṚV X.57.6) and like *karma* with primary reference to sacrificial operation (cf. Lat. *operari = sacra facere*) as is explicit in ŚB I.1.1.1 and I.9.3.23 where *vrata = yajña*. Operation is twofold, "interior" (*guhya*) and "exterior" (*dvir*). These two "operations" are essentially those of the Sacerdotium and the Regnum *in divinis*. As That One the deity is "idle" (*avrata*, cf. *ná . . . vyábhavat* in BU I.4.11, and *apravartin* CU III.12.9 and Kauṣ U. IV.8), or, as this is expressed in TS I.5.9.5, "The operations are mingled at night, the better and the worse lie down together" (*sáṁ hi náktam vratáni sṛjyántc, sahá śreyāṅś ca pāpīyāṅṣ cāsāte*) but when "proceeding to the sacrificial part" (*yajñíyam bhāgam emi*, ṚV X.124.3) "supremely operative" (*vratatama*, ṚV VIII.44.21).

Vrātya implies the potentiality of operation (JB II.233 *soman vatayati*, "puts Soma to work", i.e. drinks Soma.) Brahma, the *brahma*, is then the "One and only Vrātya", the source of the *brahma* and *kṣatra* proper to Bṛhaspati and Indra, who becomes the Lord, (*iśāna* on whom all beings attend, and arming himself with Indra's bow "covers up the hostile brotherhood" (*ápriyam bhrātṛvyam*) and "pierces him who hates" (*dviṣantam*), AV XV.1.5-6, XV.3.10, XV.10.3-6, cf. IV.1.3. Otherwise stated, the "only Vrātya is Vāyu", is the Gale of the Spirit it that blows from the four quarters as the kings Indra, Īśāna, Varuṇa and Soma and from above as Prajāpati (JUB III.21.3); or Prāṇa-Prajāpati, the Breath (Praśna Up. II.7). Thus the unmanifested *Brahma* enters into the worlds as priest and king, as Agni-Bṛhaspati and Indra; he is the archetypal "guest" and king whom his satellites welcome with the cry "Here comes *Brahma*!" (BU IV.3.37). His welcome is a kind of Rājasūya. It is natural, then, that the throne (*āsandi*) prepared for the Vrātya in AV XV.3 should resemble Brahmā's in Kaus. Up. I.5 and Indra's in AB VIII.12, and likewise the Buddha's throne in the early iconography, for all these are "guests" to be welcomed as kings.

Vrātya in the plural is, then, by analogy an epithet that can be applied to any brāhmaṇa considered as a manifestation of Brahma, or equally to any alien guest who is qualified by nature to be received into the Aryan fold and inducted into the Aryan operations (*āryā vratd*, ṚV X.65.11): we see that for the Aryan householder or king to address the stranger as a "Vrātya" (AV XV.10.1-2, 11.1-2, 12.1-2) is to pay him the highest honour and to say in effect: "We are altogether your servants". Thus the tradition of hospitality is based on metaphysical principles, hospitality is a rite, the guest is a living symbol of the deity (*Brahma* = Guest). It becomes understandable, also, why it is that a guest may be feared as well as honoured: it is an enemy that comes to be received as a friend, a Varuṇa whom one receives as a Mitra; the "welcome" is in any case a "pacification" (*śānti* from *śam*) and is a "quieting" analogous to that of the *śamitṛ* who gives the quietus to the sacrificial victim — it should not be overlooked that the proceeding deity is, in fact, himself the sacrifice (ṚV X.13.4, X.81.5, ŚB *passim*, etc.). This is especially clear in KU I.7

where the brāhmaṇa guest is called a "fire" and *tasya . . . śātiṁ* refers at the same time to the extinction of the "fire" and the pacification of the "guest", as TS V.I.6.1 where "the waters are pacifications, and with these pacifications he quiets Agni's burning anguish"(*āpo vai śāntāḥ, śāntābhir evāsya śucaṁ śamayati, śucam* corresponding to the "sharpness of the fire-flash" contrasted with the "meekness and light" in Behmen, *Three Principles*, XIV.69-77); cf. the extinction or pacification (*śānti*) of the fire in PB VIII.7.8, and the value of *śānti* in Pāli Buddhism where the extinction or pacification of the fire of life is the same as *nibbāna*. *Saṁśam* in Mbh is both to "kill" and to "make peace with", since in "making peace" we put an end to the enemy and generate a friend; it is logically impossible to make "peace with an enemy", whom like Varuṇa we can only approach when we have "made him a friend" (*mitrakṛtya*), and this passage from enmity to friendship (cf. the double entendre of *hostis*), like all other transitions, is the death of what was and a birth of what is. In BG VI.7 where the empirical self has been "overcome and pacified" (*jita praśānta*), *praśānta* has all the values of "sacrificed", "made sacred", "made holy", as in the ritual sacrifice itself, where the sacrificer is identified with the victim and called as self-sacrificer" (*ātmyāji*, ŚB XI.2.6.13, cf. I.8.3.18, etc., and Manu, XII.91).

This digression has been necessary to an understanding of *vrata*, a word that can only be rendered correctly by "operation", and equated with *karma*; it should be added that all occupations are traditionally sacrificial rites, cf. R̥V IX.112, I.2 where the vocations of the priest, the carpenter, doctor, and fletcher are all equally *vratāni*. We can now understand the full meaning of *saṁvratā* which is quite literally that of "co-operative", and that of *pativratā*, a "devoted wife"; to use a later word, the "wife", the "royal" partner, is to act as *sahadharmiṇī*, a partner in the fulfilment of the Eternal Law, which as *svadharma* becomes the Law of one's own Vocation; the analogous *ánuvaratā* in AV XIV.1.42, TS I.1.10, and JUB I.54.6, and implied in the *Arthaśāstra* I, adhy. 9. "The king should obey (*anuvarteta*, i.e. should be *anuvrata* with respect to) the *purohita*, as is a pupil to his master, a son to a father, or a serf to his feudal lord" (*svāmi*), and as might have been added, as is a wife to a husband whom she should "love, honour, and obey". Contrasted with these co-operations, the alternative of other and independent operation (*anyavrata*) would be satanic (R̥V X.22.8, VS XXXVIII.20), cf. AB II.5,

AV V.18.8-9, where "instigated by the mind the voice speaks (*manasā va iṣitā vāg vadati*), but what she utters absent mindedly is of the *asuras* and not acceptable to the gods" (*yāṁ hy anyamanā vācaṁ vadati asuryā vai sā vāg adevajuṣṭā*; the "mind" here being the sacrificial Maitrāvaruṇa, i.e. the *brahmā*, and the "voice" the *hotṛ*, functionally feminine).

32. AV III.8.5 *saṁ vo manāṅsi saṁ vratā*; TB II.4.4.4-5 *saṅgachadhvam saṁvadadhvam. saṁ vo manāṅsi jānātām. devā bhāgam yathā pūrve. saṁjānānā upāsata. samāno mantraḥ samitiḥ ṣamānī saṁānaṁ manaḥ saha cittameṣām. saṁānaṁ ketô abhi saṁrabhadhavaṁ. saṁjñānena vo haviṣā yajāmaḥ. samānī va ākūtiḥ samānā hṛdayānī vaḥ saṁānamastu vo manaḥ yathā vaḥ susahāsati*, see also ṚV X.191.2-4, X.65.8, TS IV.2.5.1, AV VI.64.1-3.

33. That the marriage of the two Agnis, *kṣatra* and *brahma*, in TS V.2.4 is a union of mutually antagonistic principles, reflects the natural opposition of Sacerdotium and Regnum and natural antagonism of the sexes. What pertains to Mitra does not pertain to Varuṇa (ŚB III.4.18): The *kṣatra* takes no delight in the *brahma*, nor does the *brahmavarcasa* delight in the *kṣatra* (ŚB XIII.1.5.2, 3); *amoris sive dilectionis radix et causa est similitudo* (Ecclesiasticus XIII.19), and as Eckhart adds, *E converso vero dissimilitudo est causa odii*. [= The root and cause of love is likeness. Conversely indeed, unlikeness is the cause of hatred.] The nature and functions of the Sacerdotium and the Regnum, like those of man and woman, are distinct: the marriage is a reconciliation that reflects their transcendental unity ("Agni is both Mitra and Varuṇa", ṚV VII.12.3; "Brahma both *brahma* and *kṣatra*", ŚB X.4.1.9; Christ "both king and priest", St. Thomas Aquinas, *Sum. Theol.* III.31.2 ad 2).

That is so many of the oldest languages the same roots embrace opposite meanings (which must be only distinguishable by the addition of determinants) is of fundamental significance for the ontology of thought. It is an indication that the movement of primitive thought deduces qualities; it is not abstractive but deductive — an indication of number. All that is essential for the adequacy of the symbolism is the mutual contrariety of related forms which are essentially of one kind, but can be divided for practical purposes. A good example of this "open sesame" motif can be cited from Southern Africa. The same synthetic bias is to be recognized in the old duals (e.g. Mitrāvaruṇau) that import, not a mere composition of two "persons" but the becoming of one.

The very word *mithunam* implies a "clash" of contraries, and *mithyā* is "false" as being contrary (to the truth). For the marriage of mutually antagonistic principles cf. AV III.8.5 "I bend together your minds, operations and intentions, ye who are of contrasted operation, these of yours I bend together" (*saṁ vo manāṅsi saṁ vratā saṁ ākutīr namāmasi, amī ye vivratā sthana tān vaḥ saṁ namayāmasi*). This is primarily, no doubt, addressed to Sky and Earth; in a hymn "for supremacy" (*śraiṣṭhye*) it would be applicable to the analogous *brahma* and *kṣatra*. The wording is closely related also to that of TS IV.2.5.1 and R̥V X.65-68 and X.191.2-4.

At the same time the kindling of Agni is the quickening and resurrection of Varuṇa: Agni becomes "his father's augmenter" (*vardhanam pituḥ,* R̥V I.140.3 and thus his "father's father", *pituṣ pitā,* R̥V VI.16.35), the Son reproducing the Father whom he displaces. The two Agnis of our texts are the one that "falls" (dies) with Soma and Varuṇa (= Cyavāna) in R̥V X.124 (*agniḥ somo varuṇas te cyavante*) and the one proceeding as God (*deváḥ*) from the No-god (*ádevāt,* i.e. from the *asura pitr̥,* now *Deus absconditus, mūra deva,* like Prajāpati, *jiryā mūraḥ* in PB XXV.17.3) from the non-sacrificial to the sacrificial part (*ayajñiyād yajñíyam bhāgám emi*) and who with a view to immortality (*prapāśyamāno amr̥tatvám*) abandons (*jáhāmi*) the Titan Father, choosing (*vr̥ṇānáḥ*) Indra; cf. R̥V IV.26.7 where Indra abandons (*ajahāt*) the senile deities (*mūráḥ*, sc. *deváḥ*), VI.47.17 where Indra rejects his former friends, who do not follow him, and seeks others, VI.59.1, "Your parents, foes of the gods, Indrāgnī, are smitten down, and ye survive", and X.69.10 where Agni, the Youngest, vanquishes the Ancients, though they were friendly. The abandonment of the Father by Indrāgnī corresponds to that of Cyavāna in JB III.77. The reversal of the kingdom (*paryávard rāṣṭrām*) in R̥V X.124 is reflected in TS VI.6.5 where Varuṇa is the type of the banished king and Indra that of the one in power, and the offering is to free oneself from what pertains to Varuṇa, for as in R̥V X.124.8 "the people who elect a king stand aloof in horror from Vr̥tra" (*vīśo ná rájānaṁ vr̥ṇānā bībhatsúvo ápa vr̥trād atiṣṭhan*), incidentally an interesting reference to the part of the people in the choice of the king: that the reference of "Vr̥tra" here is to a nature from which as regards its evil the king is to be purged, but which as regards its force is to remain in him (just as the gods retain the *ahimāyāḥ* of the *asuras*), can be seen from PB XVI.4.1-5 and XVIII.9.6, 7, where Indra puts on the lotus-wreath (*puṣkarasraja*) which his father Prajāpati (i.e Varuṇa now succeeded by his son) had had made for himself "for the sake of supremacy" (*śreṣṭhyā*) — it is "wrought of the savour of the quarters and all his offspring", its twelve flowers are the months, it is the "royal force" (*indriyaṁ vīryam*) of the Year, Prajāpati, Varuṇa — and "when he put on the lotus wreath, it is the Regnum, the very form (or aspect) of Vr̥tra, that he puts on" (*vr̥trasyaiva tad rūpaṁ kṣatram pratimuñcate*), that Vr̥tra whom, as we are reminded in the same verse, he has already slain. Similarly MS IV.4.7 where the lotus (wreath) is "the very form of the Regnum" (*kṣatrasyaiva rūpam*); and ŚB V.4.5.4 where the lotus wreath is "the form of the sky" (*divo rūpam*). The conclusion, *Vr̥tra = Dyaus = Kṣatra,* will not astonish us. The Dragonslayer assimilates the Dragon's power but not his malice, and inherits his treasure, so that Vr̥tra says to Indra: "Thou art now what I was erst" (ŚB I.6.3.17).

Thus indeed Indra "supersedes" the father (Varuṇa, Dyaus, Prajāpati, or Vr̥tra) whom he has overcome or more strictly speaking "sacrificed"; the pseudo-historial legend of his namesake Ajātaśatru is another recension of the same story. But to think of this "supersession of Varuṇa by Indra" as the refleetion of some doctrinal "evolution", or even to say that "Varuṇa was divested of his supreme powers by the time of the AV" (Macdonell, *Vedic Mythology*, pp. 65, 66) is a misapplication of "historical method" and only displays the mythologist's ignorance of theology. For Indrāgnī are liberators above all else: they bring forth their people from captivity into a promised land. And every such soteriology necessarily transfers the kingdom, whether by conquest or by a sacrificial atonement, from a "wrathful Father" to a milder Son, from the God *ab intra* to the God *ab extra,* in so far as a distinction can be made between them. So Christ says: "All power is given unto me in heaven and in earth" (Matth. XXVIII.18). What is true for the *genealogia regni dei* is true in every human lineage; the Prince who comes to the throne "supersedes" his father (whether he has been ritually "despatched" or has died by natural causes) and inherits his power (ŚB V.4.2.10), but establishes a new order. In this connection it is highly significant that one of the first acts of a new king, celebrating his accession, is a release of prisoners from jail. It is thus that Varuṇa, when his ferocity has been appeased, releases

Śunaḥśepa (ṚV I.24.11-13). It is also true for the "people" that the son "supersedes" the father and inherits his rank, as in Kauṣ. U. II.15 (10) where if the father who has made the last "bequest" by which the transmission and delegation of all his powers to his son is effected should recover, he can no more resume these powers than if he were actually dead, but must live subject to his son, or as a religious mendicant. The "supersession" of Varuṇa by Indra, or rather by the twins (*yamaū*, ṚV VI.59.2) Indrāgnī, is an ontological, not an historial event.

The proceeding Agni in ṚV X.124 leaves *himself* behind at the same time that he goes forth, as also in ṚV III.55.7 where "he proceeds in front and still remains within his ground" (*ánv ágraṁ cárati kṣeti budhnáḥ*): "the Son remains within as essence and goes forth as Person . . . the divine nature steps forth into relations of otherness . . . other, but not another, for this distinction is rational, not real" (Eckhart, Evans, ed., I.268). Nor is there any inconsistency in that, having "chosen" Indra, Agni invites his father Varuṇa to "Come forth to be the ruler of my kingdom" (ṚV X.124.5), for Varuṇa is Indra (ṚV IV.42.3) as much as he is Agni, and the Rājasūya is "Varuṇa's Quickening", or regeneration. . . . The "late" king rules in the "present".

34. Agni is Ahirbudhnya *ab intra* and Agni Gārhapatya *ab extra* (AB III.36, KB XVI.7, cf. VS V.33). ṚV abounds with references to Agni's chthonic origins from his "ground" (*budhna*, e.g. IV.I.11. *sá jáyata prathamáḥ . . . budhné* = V.3.1 *tvām agne váruṇo jāyase*) — a "ground" amongst the waters — or from the "rock" (*adri*), the "stone" (*aśman*), or "mountain" (*parvata*).

35. In connection with the "fear" and "love" of Varuṇa it should be remembered that "Nothing prevents one and the same thing being loved under one aspect and hated under another" (St. Thomas Aquinas, *Sum. Theol.* I.20.2 ad 4).

36. Or "five missiles" (Keith): to be identified, in the last analysis with the "five arrows" of Kāmadeva, bearing in mind that Love and Death, Kāma and Mṛtyu, are one and the same person.

37. It is not of his own power, but inasmuch as "God is with him" that the kṣatriya is victorious; he says, accordingly: "I destroy the unfriends and lead forth my own subjects with the help of the spiritual power" (*kṣinomi brahmaṇā mitrān unnayāmi svām*, VS XII.82

and ŚB VI.6.3.15), of which ṚV affords innumerable instances in the co-operation of Agni-Bṛhaspati with Indra against the *asuras*. We propose to show that the archetype of the unfriend or unfriends, so often referred to in the texts as "he whom we hate and who hateth us" (— is a *rākṣasa* TS VI.3.9.2), and as the "loveless brotherhood" (*apriyam bhrātṛvyam*) are primarily and in most cases Vṛtra–Varuṇa–Mṛtyu and the *asuras* generally. Quite exceptionally *bhrātṛvyatā* is "brotherly aid" in JB I.184. In ŚB IV.3.3.5 "the evil, hateful brotherhood" (*pāpmane dviṣate bhrātṛvyāya*) is explicitly Vṛtra, and in ŚB XII.7.3.4 *dviṣantam bhrātṛvyam* is Namuci, Pāpmana. In JUB I.7.2 the "evil brotherhood", to be excluded "mentally" from any share in these worlds, can only be, so to say, Satan. He has accomplished the purpose of the sacrifice who "has slain his Vṛtra" (TS II.5.4.5). So that while it is beyond question that the *purohita* sometimes assists, or rather enables, the king to overcome human enemies, the fundamental conflict is "not against flesh and blood, but against the principalities, against powers, against the rulers of the darkness of this world (New Test. *Eph.* VI.12). When it *is* a question of human enemies, these are assimilated to the Adversary himself, and the weapons effective against him are turned against them: war, from the traditional point of view, being no more than any other vocational activity, a merely profane engagement (see n. 106).

The "brotherhood" (*bhrātṛvyaḥ*, which Hume, p. 293 equates etymologically with "cousin") that is synonymous with enmity (and to be distinguished from brotherliness *bhrātṛtva*, in a favourable sense, ṚV VIII.83.8, cf. X.23.7) is, then, the relationship of the *asuras* to the *devas*, of the Varuṇa who is "not Mitra" but *amitra*, unfriend, to Agni, *mitra*, the friend. (ŚB IV.4.5.3 *asti manuṣyānāṁ ca sarpānām bhrātṛvyam iva* = there is as it were a feud between men and snakes.) Varuṇa is Agni's "elder brother" in ṚV IV.1.2: "Turn thou, O Agni, thine elder brother Varuṇa toward (or possibly, "turn thyself toward") the Sun, support of men, the king, support of men" (*sa bhrātaraṁ varuṇam agna ā vavṛtsva . . . jyeṣṭham . . . ādityaṁ carṣaṇīdhṛtaṁ, rājānaṁ carṣaṇīdhṛtaṁ*, where *ādityam* is the accusative of the person turned to, like *mā* in ŚB IV.1.4.4 *upa māvartasva* and ṚV IV.31.4 *abhī na ā vavṛtsva cakram na vṛttaṁ arvataḥ* "turn hitherwards . . ."). This is only the special case of the general rule that the *asuras* are the elder brothers of the *devas* (BU I.3.1 *kānīyasā eva devāḥ, jyāyasā asurāḥ;*

Mbh XII.33.25 *asurā bhrātaro jyeṣṭhā devāś cāpi yavīyasaḥ*), and of the principle that the "brother-hood" of "those who hate one another" is that of the *deva*s and *asura*s (TS VI.4.10.1). It is significant that the root in *jyeṣṭha* is *jyā*, with the primary meaning to "oppress", distinctly preserved in ṚV VII.86.6 *asti jyāyān kanīyasa upāre*, "the elder is at hand to hurt the younger" (the reference being to Varuṇa himself, *ārpayitṛ* in ŚB V.5.4.31): it is, in fact, the rule in folklore that the elder brothers or sisters oppress the younger brother who is always the solar hero, or younger sister who is always the bride of a solar hero.

It will be noticed that ṚV IV.1.2 cited above is rather "entropaic" than apotropaic, and that *ā vavṛtsva*, like *upa māvartasva*, is essentially an invitation to union, *saṁśrityai:* the opposite of *āvṛt*, to "turn to", is *vivṛt*, to "turn apart", as in ṚV VII.80.1 *vivartayantīm rajasī* "divorcing Sky and Earth", and ŚA VII.12 *saṅdhiṁ vivartayati*, "disjoins the grammatical fusion of syllables" (in a Saṁhitā text, the marriage of words being thought of as analogous to that of Sky and Earth, and thus life-giving, *āyuṣya*, ŚA VIII.II. For *vyāvṛtti* see TS VI.1.1.5, V.4.10.3, AB VIII.8 and *vyāvṛtya śarireṇa* ŚB X.4.3.9). The "entropy" of our texts thus annuls the "divorce" of sky and earth, essence and nature, that takes place at the "creation", or rather manifestation or utterance, of the worlds, as in ṚV VII.80.1 where the Light of Dawn "divorces the coterminous regions (sky and earth, according to Sāyaṇa, but also possibly day and night), makes manifest the several worlds" (*vivartayantī rajasī samante āviṣkṛṇvatīm bhuvanāni viśvā*), cf. ṚV VI.32.2 and ŚB IV.6.7.9. We remark in passing that the separation of the conjoint principles by Light, usually that of the early-waking or early-kindled Agni, is the motive in the equivalent story of Purūravas and Urvaśī, ŚB XI.5.1.4, and in that of Eros and Psyche.

Ā vavṛtsva, then, is a prayer for the *asura*'s conversion (cf. W.N. Brown, "Proselytising the Asuras", *JAOS* 39, 1919), as in ṚV I.25 where Varuṇa's wrath is deprecated and his mercy is lauded, and AB III.4 where Agni's Vāruṇya form is "deadly to be touched" (cf. JUB II.14 and JB I.126 Indra to Uśanas, *asinān abhyūpavartasva*) and "one should approach him only having made him Mitra" (*mitrakṛtyevopāsate*, cf. JUB VIII.74.1 *mitram iva priyam*), which is possible inasmuch as "As one approaches him, so he becomes" (*yathā-yathopāsate tad eva bhavati*, ŚB X.5.2.20). In the same way "Soma was Vṛtra" (ŚB IV.4.3.4 and TS 1.2.10.2 Soma: *sīda varuṇo 'si dhṛtavrato* [*dharmarāja*] *varuṇam asi;* as "Prajāpati was Rohita", AV XIII.2.39). "Soma when tied up (*upanaddha*) is Varuṇa" (*aśnāpinaddham* ṚV X.68.8 and TS VI.1.11 — *varuṇ iva eṣa yajamānam abhyaiti yat krītaḥ soma upanaddha* . . .) and "saying, 'Come forth as Mitra' (*mitro na ehi*) he (the priest) makes what is of Varuṇa's nature to be of Mitra's" (*yad vāruṇam santam maitraṁ karoti,* TS VI.1.11.1-2), as also in ŚB III.3.3.10, quoting VS IV.27, where Soma is besought to come forth as Mitra (*mitro na ehi* TS I.2.7); that is to say "Have mercy upon us, O Lord". In ŚB III.3.4.25, 29-30 where "Soma is now of Varuṇa's nature" (Sāyaṇa says *somo varuṇo bhavati*), he is besought "not to slay our men (*avīrahā* as in ṚV I.91.19) or do evil": the ritual slaying of Soma himself, essential to his kingship, is called a "slaughter of his evil, not of himself" (ŚB III.9.4.17-18). The Adābhya Soma draught drawn "from the tied up Soma, for (his) liberation" is the symbol of "Prajāpati the Liberator" (*atimokṣiṇī*) and, by analogy, the human sacrificer and comprehensor, who is no less than Soma himself the victim and has died with Soma as such, "is wholly liberated from the evil brotherhood" (*ati pāpmānam bhrātṛvyam mucyate,* TS VI.6.9.2 and ŚB XII.7.3.4): and here it is unmistakable that the "evil brotherhood" does not refer to any human adversary but to the Vṛtra-Varuṇa nature that was in Soma and in the sacrificer's "old man" (*druho muñcāmi varuṇasya pāśāt* AV II.10.1, 8; ŚB IV.5.7.7; for Varuṇa as redeemer from sin, see ŚB III.8.5.10 and TS III.4.11.6; Varuṇa's rope = the noose of the sacred order ŚB III.7.4.1).

Soma is not destroyed by his "death", but "made to go alive to the world of heavenly-light", and in the same way the sacrificer by his death with Soma goes alive to the world of heavenly-light (TS VI.6.9.2); furthermore, "he gains through him (Soma) this All, and there is no slayer, no deadly shaft for him by whom this All has been gained" (ŚB III.3.4.9), that is to say he wins the "human immortality" here and "incorruptible immortality" hereafter, as explained in n. 53.

Although our immediate problem has been that of the identification of the "evil brotherhood", we cannot refrain from pointing out here that there are the closest possible parallels between the Indian and the Christian sacrifices, and that the Indian doctrine is not merely like, but, with only the substitution of the "Agni" for "Christ" (a merely nominal difference; and, in this connection the etymological equivalence of (anointed =)χριστος-*Christos* and *ghṛta** is not without interest), identical with that of N.T. Rom. VI.5-9: "For if we have been planted together (Gr. *symphytoi* for which Liddell and Scott's first meaning is "born with one", i.e. coborn, *sajāta, sayoni,* and of the same parentage with him) in the likeness of his death, we shall be also in the likeness of his resurrection: "Knowing this, that our old man is crucified (sacrified) with him, that the body of sin might be destroyed, that hence forth we might not serve sin. For he that is dead is freed from sin. Now if we be dead with Christ, we believe that we shall also live with him: Knowing that Christ being raised from the dead dieth no more (*jam non moritur = na punar mriyate*); death hath no more dominion over him". "Planted together" is of particular interest here, and might better have been rendered by "sown together"; we recognize the usual symbol of agriculture, in which the womb is the field into which the man, whether in natural or in supernatural generation, sows himself, and from which he springs up again (John XII.24, "Except a corn of wheat fall into the ground *and die,* it abideth alone: but if it die, it bringeth forth much fruit"). Now, just as the natural insemination is a death and a regeneration (JUB III.8.10 and 9.1, etc.), so is the supernatural, where the sacrificial fire is the womb and it is inasmuch as the sacrificer "inseminates himself (*ātmānaṁ siñcati*) therein that he comes to birth in yonder Sun and is possessed of two selves (*dvyātman,* JB I.17.6, cf. AB VI.29 and ŚB VII.2.1.6), of which the second is, of course, the "new man", the *anyam ātmānaṁ* of ŚB IV.3.4.5. And just as in natural generation the newborn son is a rebirth of the father, so here that "other self" of the "new man" is a regeneration of the "old man" that was sacrificed (made holy) together with the deity, who is the sacrifice. It is the "old man's" evil, not himself that is slain; the "death of the soul" is not a destruction of anything but its evil, nothing but the annihilation of what is already negative; in the agricultural symbolism it is only the husk of the grain that is left behind, not the germ that springs up again. The new man that thus springs up is at once the son of the old man and a son of God; and it is with reference to the first of these affiliations (both implied by St. Paul's *symphytoi*) that Eckhart, distinguishing the accidental features of the natural man from the

---

* "Let us declare aloud the name of *ghṛta*!" — VS XVII.90; ṚV IV.58.6-11.

essence of the other and new man, says that "He who sees *me*, sees *my child*" (Evans, I.408; Pfeiffer, p. 593 and Rūmī, *Mathnawī*, I-3511 "The body, like a mother, is big with the spirit-child"). But to see *that* self requires other eyes than those of the flesh (cf. Hermes, *Lib.* XIII.3 and S. I.23).

To return to "Varuṇa and what is Vāruṇya": it is Varuṇa that seizes (*gṛhṇāti*) the sick man (TS II.3.11.1; V.2.1.3; AB VII.15), the sacrificer's children (TS VI.6.5.4; MS I.10.2; ŚB II.3.2.10) and "whatever is seized by the Evil One" — or "by evil" — (*yaḥ pāpmanā gṛhīto bhavati*, ŚB XII.7.2.17), i.e. Indra's mortal enemy, "the overweening foe" (*abhimāti*) of TS II.1.2.5 and ṚV III.51.3 (cf. *abhimāno devo varuṇaḥ*, Sāyaṇa on ṚV I.89.3 Agni and Indra, *per contra*, are *sumanas*, ṚV passim). It is inasmuch as he thus "seizes" that he is "the seizer" (*graha*, JUB IV.1.7, etc.), an epithet of sinister connotation and a synonym of *makara* = *śiśumāra* and *jhaṣa* (√*jhaṣ*, to injure). It is with the "noose of Order" (*ṛtasyaiva pāśena*) that one binds (*pratimuñcati*) the sacrificial victim, and "that cord is Varuṇa's" *varuṇyā vā eṣā yad rajjuḥ*, ŚB III.7.4.1). The Vedas, e.g. ṚV I.24.11; I.25.1-2 abound with the fear of Varuṇa and the deprecation of his murderous wrath; the wages of sin is death and vengeance is his, to repay. In ŚA XII.21 and 28 we find an amulet worn by the sacrificer "in order that the celestial Varuṇa (*divyo varuṇaḥ*, i.e. Dyaus, *varuṇo dyaur iva* in ṚV VII.87.6) may not strike fear into him (*nainam. . . . hanti bhītam*). . . and Varuṇa does not slay him in his pride, neither does the *makara*, or *graha* or *śiśumāra* hurt him". On the other hand, when the peace-offering has been made, when the *asura* has been "converted" and "made a friend of", then it is not "Varuṇa" but the *mixta persona* of Mitrāvaruṇau that accepts the sacrificer (ṚV I.25.6): "By means of Mitra he (the priest) appeases (*śamayati*, slays, sacrifices) Varuṇa for him (the sacrificer) . . . sets him free (*muñcati*) from Varuṇa's noose, so that even if his life be almost gone (*yádī 'tāsur bhávati*, not Keith's "if his life *be* gone" but "if it be *becoming* gone") he verily lives" (TS II.1.9.3): and in the same way that the royal sacrificer himself, assimilated to Prajāpati (the *atimokṣiṇī* of TS VI.6.9.2), and by means of the barley offering, "delivers his children (subjects) from Varuṇa's noose (*prajá varuṇapāśāt prámuñcati*), and those children of his are born sound and sinless (*tá asyánamīva ákilbiṣāḥ prajāḥ prajāyante*), saying: 'It is in order that my children may be born sound and sinless that I would be quickened'" (*abhisūye*, ŚB V.2.4.2; V.2.5.16; II.5.2.2.3), cf. ṚV X.97.16 *varuṇ śāt . . . yamasya páḍvīśāt sárvasmād devakilviṣát*, where the assimilation of Varuṇa to Yama is unmistakable, and we see also why it is that the prince must be *reborn* to the Kingship, and for what he aspires to dominion.

As to the "barley-offering" we learn from KB V.3 that when Prajāpati's children "have been expressed" (*sṛṣṭāḥ*) but are still unquickened (*aprasūtāḥ*, not viable, not alive, unborn, cf. *na jāyante* in Avyakta U. VI.I, *JAOS* 60.349) but "are eating of Varuṇa's barley" (*varuṇasya yavāṁ cakṣuḥ*), it is Varuṇa that "restrains them with his nooses" (*vāruṇo varuṇapāśaiḥ pratyamuñcat*), and that it is only when he has been "endeared" (*prītaḥ*, i.e. made a friend, *mitra*) that he frees them from these nooses of Varuṇa and all evil (*varuṇa-pāśebhyaḥ sarvasmāc ca pāpmanaḥ prajāḥ prāmuñcat*, ŚB II.5.2.2-5). Varuṇa's barley is the "pasturage" (*yavasa*) from which they who are like kine without a herdsman (*gāvo ná . . . āgopāḥ*), yet are intent upon (or trust) the friend (*abhi mitráṁ citásaḥ*), escape (*īyuḥ*, ṚV VII.18.5-10): these same "kine, led forth, eat of the Ari's (Indra's) barley (*gávo yávam práyutā aryó akṣan*); I have seen them as they came forth, (now) in a Herdsman's care" (*sahágopāḥ*, ṚV X.27.8). Varuṇa's barley, the food of the unborn, suggests the "flesh-pots of Egypt", a correlation that corresponds to that of Varuṇa-Vṛtra with Pharoah". (My suggested rendering of *citásaḥ* above by "who trust" depends upon the fact that *vicikitsā* is the contrary of *śraddhā*, from which it follows that to "trust in" or "trow on" is a meaning that pertains to $\sqrt{cit}$, cf. *cétyaḥ* in ṚV VI.1.5.).

We have elsewhere (JAOS 55.409-10) identified Varuṇa and the Vāruṇya Agni with Ahi-Vṛtra-Śuṣṇa-Namuci, and these with the Pharoah of Ezekiel XXIX.3, "The great dragon that lieth in the midst of the rivers, which has said, My river is my own, and I have made it for myself". *Pitáram jahámi* in ṚV X.124.4 makes of the *asura* father, who is also the "elder brother" (*pitā, jyeṣṭho bhrātā vā*, Sāyaṇa on ṚV X.20.7), an "Ahi" in the sense of JB III.77 *yad ahīyata, tad ahīnām ahitvam:* and actually, the prior and fiercer form, which Agni abandons when he is kindled, is an Ahi (Ahi Budhnya, AB III.36, KB XVI.7, Ahi Dhuni, ṚV I.79.1).

Varuṇa and Vṛtra derive alike from $\sqrt{vṛ}$ to "cover" and "restrain" (*Nirukta*, X.3; BD II.33; Grassmann, *Wörterbuch;* and cf. ṚV VI.75.18 *urorvarīyo varuṇaḥ*, VII.82.6 where Varuṇa *pra vṛṇoti*, Sāyaṇa's gloss on ṚV I.89.3 *vṛnoti svakīyaiḥ pāśair āvṛṇotīti, rātry abhimāno devo varuṇaḥ*, and GB I.7, *varaṇa* as Varuṇa): i.e., inasmuch as Mitra is the

Day and Varuṇa the Night, the Darkness (TS I.3.11 *dhāmno dhāmno rājannitô varuṇa no muñca, yadāpo aghniyā varuṇeti śapāmahe tato varuṇa no muñca* = From every rule of thine, O King Varuṇa, set us free; from whatever oath by the waters, by the kine, by Varuṇa, we have sworn, From that, O Varuṇa, set us free), i.e. Evil, Death, cf. also TS II.1.7.4; TB 1.7.10; and Mādhava on TS I.8.16.1; TS V.7.5.1; AB IV.5. *Muñca* would suggest Varuṇa is by nature *na-muci,* non-dying.

"We are thus led to assimilate Varuṇa, not to the vanquishers of the demons, but to the demons themselves. . . . This is the severe aspect of the Divinity, which his name proclaims in advance" (Bergaigne, *La Religion Védique,* III.115): The epithet *asura* is . . . specially applicable to Varuṇa" (Macdonell, *Vedic Mythology,* p. 24), as is that of Deva to Savitṛ.

It is in connection with the withholding of the waters by Varuṇa and their release by Indra that the assimilation of Varuṇa to Śuṣṇa and Vṛtra is most apparent; we must not be confused by the fact that, when associated with Mitra, Varuṇa becomes a "rain-god". It is to Varuṇa that stagnant waters pertain, for they are "seized" (*gṛhīta*) by him as their *graha,* while it is the flowing waters, "living waters", divine and fit for sacrificial use that Indra frees from Vṛtra (TS II.3.13.2 seizure by Varuṇa's noose is seizure "by evil", *pāpmanā;* also TS VI.4.2.3; ŚB IV.4.5.10, etc.). The opposition of Indra to Varuṇa and the assimilation of the latter to Vṛtra are conspicuous in AV III.13.1-2 where the waters "go forth together (*samprayatīḥ*) when Ahi is smitten (*ahau . . . haté*). . . . When sent forth by Varuṇa (*yat préṣitāḥ varuṇena*) . . . then Indra obtained you" (*tad āpnod indro vaḥ*) and it is evident that Varuṇa only releases the waters when *he,* Ahi, has been smitten. ("In the very remarkable song [ṚV X.124.7] Vṛtra seems to have been actually put in the place of Varuṇa, the old Moon-God". — E. Diecke, *Indra's Drachenkamf,* Berlin, 1905, p. 16). Another, and rather remarkable evidence for the equation Vṛtra = Varuṇa is afforded by a correlation of ŚB I.6.4.18-19 (cf. KB III.5) with ŚB II.4.4.17-19. In the first of these passages the solar Indra swallows up the lunar Vṛtra on the "night of cohabitation" (*amāvāsyā,* new moon night). In the last, the light Moon is Varuṇa, the dark Moon Mitra (so-called by assimilation, in accordance with ŚB X.6.2.1 where, in connection with Sun and Moon, it is explicit that the eaten is called by the name of the eater); and these two being a couple (*mithunam*), Mitra (the Sun) inseminates Varuṇa (the Moon). From this it follows also that Vṛtra-Varuṇa (Moon) is Indra-Mitra's (Sun's) wife; a conclusion by no means at variance with Varuṇa's femininity elsewhere or with the equation of Vṛtra and *kṣatra* in PB XVIII.9.6, and notably in agreement with ṚV X.85.29 "Potentiality (*kṛtyā*) hath gotten feet (i.e., put off her ophidian nature; cf. I.152.3 and III.55.14), and as a wife inhabits (*ā . . . viśate,* cf. JUB I.33.6 *ādityam praviśati*) her Lord" (the Sun). We see again that marriage is a reconciliation of hostile principles, involving the death (and regeneration) of the enemy as such; that there are more ways than one of "killing" a dragon; and that the *vajra* (thunderbolt) being a "shaft" of light, and "light the progenitive power" (TS VII.1.1.1; *principium motus et vitae* [= the beginning of motion and life], Witelo, *Lib. de intelligentiis* IX, etc.), the piercing of Vṛtra is also a fertilization, to be equated with that of the "lightning-smitten" Semele by Zeus.

Varuṇa is equated to Mṛtyu. By extracting from the limbs (*aṅga*) of Mṛtyu their sap (*rasa*) the final result, *aṅgiras,* is reached. The origin of *aṅgiras* is from the bitter waters of the ocean, that is, from Varuṇa who is taken here without doubt in his occasional sinister, demonic sense, as of Vṛtra, cf. Abel Bergaigne: *La Religion Védique* III.144 and Geldner *Vedische Studien,* II.292.

The Varuṇa into whose maw the Seven Rivers flow (*yasya te sapta sindhavaḥ* ṚV VIII.69.12 and "ruler of the seven rivers" ṚV VIII.41.9) is the Varuṇa that lies in wait against the current of the river, to seize the sacrificer's children (the subjects of the king; TS VI.6.5.4), the "Infanticide" (*śiśumāra* or *-mārin,* TA II.19 *parabrahma* lauded as *śiśumāra* and *śiśukumāra*), Indra's enemy, who lies against the current with yawning jaws ready to seize the sacrificer himself, and must be appeased (PB VIII.6.8; XIV.5.15; JB I.174; III.193, and TS V.1.6.8 where Agni, as Varuṇa, "attacks" the sacrificer, and ŚB IX.4.2.15-17 where Agni completed = Varuṇa): the dessication of this same Śiśumāra by Indra, who forces him upstream (cf. the apotropaic *punaḥ sarām* in AV IV.17.2 *pratikūlam* in X.1.7 and *pratisara* in ŚA XII.30) onto the dry land where he "is left, as it were" (*hīna iva,* cf. JB III.77 cited above) and his subsequent resurrection when he praises Indra who then enables him to return to the sea (JB III.173), as in the "Flood Legend" Manu rescues the tiny Jhaṣa and enables it to return to the sea (ŚB I.8.1.6), and as in the Alexander legend (see *Ars Islamica,* I, 1934, pp. 177-78), narrates in other words the inveteration and rejuvenation, death and resurrection, of Cyavana, Prajāpati, Varuṇa.

Notable for Varuṇa's connection with death is the fact that the creaking of the axle of the bodily vehicle is a sign of death (BU IV.3.35), and when the axle creaks, this "is Varuṇa of the evil voice" (*durvāk,* TS 2.9.1; cf. JUB I.52.8): that he is addressed as "sweet-voiced" (*suvāk* is "to pacify him" (*śāntyai* ib.) and corresponds to the "making him Mitra" in other contexts (But "axle creaks favourably, as Voice of Trees", in PB VI; and "Voice of Brahma utters Damayantī's name in creaking of axle", in Naiṣadhīya Carita II.50; cf. also "axle not oiled" TS II.6.3.3, and Parmenides in Sextus Emp. *Adv.Doz.* III). It is an *asura* that speaks in the creaking axle (ŚB III.5.3.17 and VI.8.1.10; AB IV.7). A *rākṣasa* that infests the car (TS V.2.2.3), whereas Agni's car is silent (R̥V I.74.7). It is repeatedly stated that what is "ill-sounding" (*apadhvāntam,* JUB I.52.8; CU II.22.1) pertains to Varuṇa; and this agrees with the distinction of *kṣatra* from *brahma* as that of the toneless (cacophonous) *r̥c* from the chanted and harmonious *sāman.* Whatever is inauspicious, inadequate, or evil is referred to Varuṇa (TS VI.6.7.3; cf. VII.3.11.1 *yo 'smān dveṣṭi*), or to Trita (R̥V VIII.47.13-14) who as Agni *ab intra,* the Vāruṇya Agni, is Varuṇa (R̥V VIII.41.6).

If Agni and Soma "when constricted" (*upanaddha*) are of Varuṇa's nature, this agrees with the close connection of nooses (*pāśa*), bonds (*baddha, dāman*), and knots (*granthi*) with Varuṇa. Thus the knot (see *sarpabandha*) is inauspicious and distinctively Varuṇa's (ŚB I.3.1.16; V.2.5.17; TS V.2.9.1), the "untying of Agni" is a dissipation of Varuṇa's wrath (TS V.1.6.1): while on the other hand Indra is the archetype (cf. JISOA, December 1935, pp. 5-6) of that Mahāvīra, Jina and Tīrthaṅkara ("Great Hero", "Conqueror" and "Ford-finder": for the last epithet cf. R̥V VI.18.5 where *indro gādhāny akr̥ṇot,* and further references in W.N. Brown, *Walking on the Water*) whose followers are expressly Nirgranthas, "Freed of the Knot", surely that "knot of Śuṣṇa's that Indra resolves" (*vi śuṣṇasya saṁgrathitam . . . vidat,* R̥V X.61.13), the Gordian knot that Soma is enjoined to untie in R̥V IX.97.18; X.143.2, and all those knots that are called "Knots of the Heart" (*hr̥daya granthiḥ,* cf. Aristotle Met. III.I.I; and Crooke, *Popular Religion and Theology of the Navaho Indians,* II.46 on cords and knots; J. Heckenbach, *De miditate sacra sacrisgue vinculis,* Giessen, 1911). Now what is it to be freed from the knot? In the first place, to be released from Varuṇa's noose so as to be born and to receive a name and shape (*nāma rūpa*). But this is only a loosening, not an unloosening of the knot; for names themselves are knots (AA II.1.6), and "everything here is gripped by name" (*nāmnā . . . gṛhītam*, ŚB IV.6.5.3). To be wholly "freed of the knot" is to be released from "name and shape", and to have "gone home" (Muṇḍ. Up. III.2.8 *nāmarūpād vimuktaḥ parātparam puruṣamupaiti divyam;* Sn. 1074 *nāmakāyā vimutto attham paleti*).

The foregoing is far from exhaustive of the material relative to Varuṇa's evil nature (PB XXIV.18 Varuṇa opposed to *deva*), i.e. to the Divine Majesty, or Wrath of God, considered apart from the Divine Mercy, to the Divine Darkness considered apart from and as opposed to the Divine Light, to Non-being and Unreality as logically distinguished from Being and Reality. It has been shown what is the nature of the "hostile brotherhood" from which the Regnum in alliance with the Spiritual Authority redeems itself in the sacrifice.

We must, at the same time briefly indicate that the whole conception is reversible, for what is "night" from the human point of view is "day" from that of the sage (BG II.69), what seems untrue or unreal to men is true and real to the Gods, the way to heaven is countercurrent, the *via affirnativa* in which the aspects of deity are distinguished must be followed by the *via negativa* in which they are all one. Love and Death are one and the same power, and to one who knows how to approach him, "making him a friend" (*mitrakṛtya*), he is the friend, Mitra as much as he is Varuṇa, and we can ask impatiently: "When at last shall we come again to be in Varuṇa? " (ṚV VII.86.2); love casting out fear.

38. This is the usual hermeneia of *sāman*. That they (He and She, Sky and Earth) united (*sametya*) and brought forth the Chant is the quiddity of the Chant" (JUB I.51.2, AB III.23, etc.). "He" (*ama*) is in various contexts Agni, Vāyu, Āditya, Candra, *kṛṣṇa, prāṇa, manas, ātman, sat, sāman;* and "she" *sā*), Iyam (Earth), Antarikṣa (Air), Dyaus (Sky) — the three "domains" — *nakṣatrāni, śukla, apāna, vāc, cakṣus, śrotra* (cf. BU I.4.17), *asat, ṛc* (JUB I.53, CU I.6.7, etc.); and all these are aspects of the Sacerdotium and Regnum respectively.

39. JUB in terms of Sky and Earth, brother and sister, supplies the "happy ending" to Yama's abortive wooing by Yamī in ṚV X.10, where, for example, *anyám icchasva . . . pátim* in verse 10 corresponds

to *anyatra mithunam icchasva* in JUB I.53.6. "Yama's rejection of 'Yamī' represents only one side of the mutual "horror" of one another felt by the conjoint principles, divided *ab extra,* and because of which "she" shrinks from "him" as often and as much as he from her, at the same time that each desires the other. All this pertains to the archetypal "psychology of sex". The pattern of Indian ontology — *itihāsa* as *purāvṛttaprātipādakam* or *sṛṣṭipratipādakam brāhmaṇam,* Sāyaṇa on ŚB XI.5.6.8, i.e. the *bhāvavṛtta* hymns of ṚV — is immeasurably less multifarious than has been supposed by those who consider "only the names" (S. I.11). In the last analysis, "The Mother and the Father and the Child are this All" (ŚA VII.15), "this Earth is the womb of Everything" (ŚB IV.1.2.8), Eve is the "mother of all living" (Gen. II.20). The stories of Śiva and Pārvatī in the *Kumārasambhava,* and that of Purūravas and Urvaśī in the *Vikramorvaśī* are just as much as the legend of Yama and Yamī versions of one and the same Liebesgeschichte Himmels (= Love story of the Heavens).

Who then are Yama and Yamī? We propose to show that they are not *sui generis,* but Sky and Earth, Day and Night, Indrāgnī, the Aśvins, the Sacerdotium and Regnum, *dampatī* and all other *dvandvas* ["Twins" (*Jāmī*) in ṚV I.159.4]. As a preliminary to this argument we must point out that "Yama" alone means "Twins" (du.), i.e. Yama and Yamī, just as Sāma is Sāma and Ṛc, Prajāpati *manas* and *vāc,* Agni born *brahma* and *kṣatra,* and *pati-patnī* one in the single androgynous Person before their schism: and that duals such as *pitarau, mātarau, svasā* are no more than *jāmáyaḥ* in ṚV X.10.10 necessarily couples of one and the same sex but nearly always pairs of opposite sex, "father and mother" (cf. *dampatī*) "brother and sister", etc. Thus in ṚV III.54.7 where Sky and Earth are *svāsārā,* I.185.5 where they are *svāsārā jāmīpitror upāsthe,* and I.159 where they are explicitly a Father *and* a Mother, whose respective natures are those of *manas,* "Intellect", and *svatavas* = *dakṣa,* "Power", having a progeny (*prajā*), but also referred to as *mātarā,* "parents", and as *jamí sáyonī mithunā sámokasá,* "uterine twins, consorts cohabitant"; it is obvious that *svásárā* and *jāmī* can only be "twin brother and sister", and at the same time impossible not to recognize the Yama and Yamī of ṚV X.10.4-5 *paramáṁ jāmi tán nau . . . garbhé . . . dámpatī.* In ṚV VIII.60.1 the reference of *mātróḥ* is not to Agni's "mothers" but to his "parents", the firesticks, which are always thought of as male and female and may be addressed as Purūravas and Urvaśī, and similarly in R̥V VI.49.2 that of *yuvatyóḥ* is not to "two young mothers" but to Father Sky and Mother Earth. In R̥V VI.59.2 Indrāgnī are *bhrātarā . . . yamaś* which can be taken to mean "twin brothers" from one point of view, but equally "twin brother and sister" when the relation of *brahma* to *kṣatra* is emphasized; in the same verse the *ihéhamātarā* are not the usual "parents" but "two mothers, here and there" on whom Indrāgnī are begotten by their one father (these "mothers", Sāyaṇa's Aditi and Earth, are Eckhart's "Mary ghostly and Mary in the flesh"). It is strange that much of this should have been overlooked by Hopkins (*JAOS* 16.cxlvi) and others who, while always ready to render *pitarau* and *mātarau* by "parents" (m. and f.) invariably render *svasārā* by "sisters", regardless of the fact that the relationship of Sky to Earth is never that of sister to sister (except as *vinatā* and *kadrū*) or brother to brother, but that of brother to sister, father to daughter, and husband to wife.

Yama, who is regularly identified with Agni, may take Agni's place as coborn twin (*yamo ha jāta indreṇa saha — Nirukta,* X.21), Indra then clearly replacing Yamī, Earth, as Yama's bride (ŚB VII.2.1.10; TS III.3.8.3, "Yama is Agni, Yamī the Earth"), quite in agreement with AB III.38 where "Indra is This (Earth) . . . the King of Being is This (Earth)", and AV XIV.1.48 where the Earth is Agni's bride.

The Aśvins, another pair of twins, may be only another form of the two pairs (*śyenau* in R̥V and described as "horse faced" cf. Gopinath Rao, *Elements of Hindu Iconography,* vol. 4, p. 544) already mentioned and collated. It can hardly be doubted that the Aśvins, twins "born here and there, one of ye Sumakha's lordly conqueror, the other Subhaga, son of Sky" (*iheha jātā . . . jiṣṇur vāmanyaḥ sumakhasya sūrirdivo anyaḥ subhagaḥ putra uhe,* R̥V I.181.4), must be identified with the twins Indrāgnī "whose mothers are here and there" (*ihehamātarā,* R̥V VI.59.2), and of whom one in his capacity as Mahāvīra and Jina is certainly "Good Makha's conqueror" (or sacrificer, Makha being the Sacrifice, and Sūriḥ implying Maghavan; see the fuller references in *JAOS* 55.377-82), and the other as the Sun certainly "Good Bhaga". That the Aśvins ride in a common chariot (*rathyeva vīrājeva yamā* R̥V II.39.2, *samānayojano hi vāṁ rathaḥ* I.30.18) again suggests Indrāgnī (*sarathaṁ tasthivāṅsā,* R̥V I.108.1, *samāné ā rathe,* VI.59.5) and likewise Kr̥ṣṇa and Arjuna (BG , cf. n. 5). That the Aśvins are referred to in R̥V II.39.1.3 as "two Brahmās" (*brāhmaṇā*) and as "two Śakras" (*śakrā*, cf. *Nirukta* XII.I, *rājānau*), and in TA I.10 as "two horses", day and night, etc. as a "pair", may well be an allusion to Indrāgnī who are both "priests" (*indro brahmā*, ṚV VIII.16.7, cf. ŚB IV.6.6.5; JUB I.45.1) and both "kings" (*indrā nu āgnī . . . vajriṇā. . . devā*, ṚV VI.59.3, etc.); the emendation *cakrā* for the *śakrā* of ṚV II.39.3 is quite unnecessary, however plausible in view of ṚV X.10.7 where Yama and Yamī are "two wheels" (i.e. Sky and Earth, Day and Night, Manas and Vāc, as wheels of the cosmic and sacrificial chariot, cf. ṚV I.30.19; VIII.89.4; AB V.30, 33; JUB I.20.3; III.16.1.2; ŚB II.3.3.12; and BD VII.126 Sun and Moon, *Prāṇāpānau*, Day and Night, or *rodasī* of ṚV VIII.70.5 and X.65.5). The Aśvins are again *śakrā* in ṚV X.24.4-5, where Sāyaṇa is absolutely right in referring *samīcī*, "the conjoint" (Sky and Earth), to the Aśvins themselves and in saying that *niramanthatam*, "ye churned" has for its object an implied *agnim;* that they thus bring Agni to birth is "at the prayer of the joyless" (*vimada*), i.e. "for the sake of Atri-Vimada" (*atraye... vimadāya*, ṚV I.51.3), cf. Trita's (Agni's, *trito guhyena vratena*, ṚV I.163.3) appeals to Sky and Earth in ṚV I.105, and Trita in the womb (ṚV X.46.6): that is to say, then, at the prayer of Agni himself as yet unborn but longing to be born, eager for the sacrificial role and choosing Indra for his ally, as in ṚV X.124.3, 4. In ṚV VI.11.1 where Agni is besought to "turn hitherward" (*ā no mitrāvaruṇā nāsatyā dyāvā hotrāya pṛthivī vavṛtyāḥ*), Mitrāvaruṇā (which are *samrājā* in ṚV X.65.5 and *hotārā* in ṚV X.66.13), the Aśvins, and Sky and Earth, these are not six different essences but three aspects of one pair; that the same deity may be referred to in one and the same context by different names, as was observed by Hopkins, *Epic Mythology*, p. 82, could be amply illustrated from ṚV, e.g. I.32.5 where *vṛtra*, *vyaṁsa*, and *ahi* are not three different persons, and X.62.11 where the *manu* of **a** is the *sāvarṇi* of **b** the reference being to Vivasvat's son by Saraṇyu's *savarṇā*, and by the same token to the Manu Vivasvati of ṚV VII.52.1. If ṚV III.54.7, speaking of Sky and Earth as "brother and sister" (*svasārā* — like Zeus and Hera) goes on to say that "they call each other by conjugal names" (*bruvāte mithunāni nāma*) — *dvandvanāma*, as Sāyaṇa, says — these can only be any or all of the names appropriate to any pair of "mates" (*mithunā*) or any of the "pairs of opposites" (*dvandvānī*) such as the two chariot wheels, or day and night, or well-done and ill-done of Kauṣ. Up. I.4; in other words, just such dual names as are descriptive of the Aśvins in ṚV II.39, names that are equally applicable to Sky and Earth, Yama and Yamī, or Sacerdotium and Regnum, or any other twin couples. In R̥V II.39 the Aśvins are compared to many such "pairs" of which some (*cakravākeva dampatī*, cf. AV XIV.2.64) are expressly and others (*grāvāṇā, akṣī* [ŚB XII.9.1.12 "two men in the eyes"], *vātā oṣṭhau,* and *kṣāmā = dyāvāpr̥thivī*) parabolically of opposite sex. *Śakrā* can as well be "King and Queen" and "two kings" (this holds equally for *rājānā* in R̥V.X.61.23, where the reference is to Mitra and Varuṇa who are, as we shall show, related to one another as man to woman). *Akṣī* "two eyes", suggest the Sun and Moon (the two cups, Sun and Moon are the eyes of the sacrifice TS VI.4.10.2-3 and *cakṣuṣī candrasūryau* Muṇḍ Up. II.1.4; Moon = Viṣṇu's left eye in *Naiṣadhacarita* 22, 89), *divo . . . akṣī* in R̥V I.72.10, respectively the god-world and man-world (JUB III.13.12), or again Indra and Indrāṇī (ŚB X.5.2.11-16). *Grāvāṇā* and *oṣṭhau,* "the upper and the nether millstones" and "upper and lower lip", are sometimes symbols of Sky and Earth; to which *kṣāmā* in any case refers. *Vātā,* "two winds" or "two breaths", corresponds to *prāṇā,* i.e. *prāṇāpānau,* in TS VI.4.9.4, the two breaths that are so often equated with Mitra and Varuṇa, Sky and Earth, and considered male and female; T.A G. Rao, *Elements of Hindu Iconography,* II.543, speaks of a personification of the Aśvins as *prāṇa* and *apāna.* An equation of the Aśvins with Sky and Earth, Yama and Yamī (i.e. Indra as Indrāṇī), *brahma* and *kṣatra,* suggests a sexual differentiation at least in principle. In this connection it may well be significant that the Egyptian Zodiacal "Twins", who correspond to the Greek Dioscuroi with whom the Aśvins have often been equated, are explicitly and iconographically of opposite sex (Wallis Budge, *Gods of the Egyptians*).

That the Aśvins (cf. Dioscuroi, Euripides, *Electra* 1350f) are regularly "saviours" (*devanam baddhamucau, rakṣitārā, tārake*) from bonds and fetters (*baddha, pāśa*) — R̥V II.39.6; AV III.7.4; JB III.72, etc. — is their function as "physicians", because of which they are in need of purification (TS VI.4.9.12; ŚB IV.1.5.13); just like the conjoint principles Sky and Earth, etc., whose elaborate purifications are described in JUB I.50-57 where it is impossible not to recognize that they are Yama and Yamī. R̥V I.109.4 invokes Indrāgnī as "Aśvins", and we see no more reason to explain this away by saying that the word means only "horsemen" in this context than to argue that in R̥V X.61.14-16, where Agni and Indra, priest and king are called *nāsatyau,* anything but the "Aśvins" is meant. R̥V VII.72.3 implied also in III.58.1 identifies the Aśvins with Sky and Earth by apposition (*ródasī dhiṣṇyemé achā vipro nāsatyā,* cf. VI.II.I *nāsatyā dhyāvā hotrāya pṛthivī vavṛtyāḥ*).

There is a side of the problem connected with the birth of the Aśvins, to which we have so far merely alluded. We must bear in mind that the word Yama means "twins", and therefore as Sāyaṇa clearly states, means Yama *and* Yamī. Now Yama is born of the Sun (Vivasvat; in Mbh XII.208.17, Mārtaṇḍa) and Tvaṣṭṛ's daughter Saraṇyū, who forthwith made off (ṚV X.17.1). This is evidently the same thing as the birth of Yama and Yamī from their "parents" in ṚV X.10.5, viz. from "the *Gandharva* in the Waters and the Maid of the Waters" (*āpyā . . . yóṣā* = Apsaras = Saraṇyū) of ṚV X.10.4. The gods concealed the immortal (bride) from mortals is another way of saying that she disappeared, as aforesaid; and they made her "like" or "double" (*savarṇā*) who bore the Aśvins, and we are told that Saraṇyū deserted "both mates" (*dvá mithunā,* ṚV X.17.2, an indication I think of the Aśvin's opposite sex, cf. ṚV II.39.2 *dámpatīva;* but cf. Whitney on AV XVIII.2.33 and Griffith's version of ṚV X.17.2). In BD VI.162 Yama and Yamī are twins, Yama the "elder" (*jyāyas*): Saraṇyū bears them, and then expressing (*sṛṣṭvā*) a woman "like" herself, entrusts the couple (*mithunau*) to this pseudo-Saraṇyū and herself makes off in the form of a mare; unaware of the deception, Vivasvat begets Manu (Manu Vaivasvata, ṚV VIII.52.1; Manu Sāvarṇi, ṚV X.62.9, 11) on the pseudo-Saraṇyū, and then, realizing what has happened, pursues the mare and begets the Aśvins, whose equine designation is thus explained.

Are the Aśvins spirit and soul? See ṚV I.164: immortal brother of the mortal".

We have thus to do with two, or three, pairs of "twins"; for Manu "Man", is as much as "Adam" a syzygy, and becomes the father of mankind by his "daughter" Parśu ("Rib", ṚV X.85.23) or Iḍā (ŚB I.8.10, etc.). The other versions of the story are discussed by Bloomfield (*JAOS* 15.172 ff.): the most noteworthy point in some of these is the term "shadow" (*chāyā*) used instead of the word "likeness" (*savarṇā*); in VP III.2 also, this "shadow" is the mother of Manu Sāvarṇi.

The expression "shadow" is significant, and enables us to make some interesting comparisons. In GB I.3 Brahma, having expressed the Waters, "sees his shadow in them" (*tāsu svāṁ chāyām apaśyat*), and his seed falls and is "supported" there; cf. the birth of Vasiṣṭha in ṚV VII.33.11 and that of Vāmadeva in PB VII.8.1, where *paryapaśyatām* corresponds to *chāyām apaśyat*. The "Shadow" in the Waters is evidently the same as the *apsaras*, "she who moves in the Waters". There are remarkable parallels in Egyptian and Greek mythology. The Egyptian Zodiacal "Twins" mentioned above are the children of the solar Śu or Tem (Amen-Rā), whose "Shadow", who is also Mother-Earth, is his wife (Budge, op. cit., I.87 f. and II.315). The Greek Centaurs, who are certainly "horse-men", are the children of Ixion (whose solar and, like Vivasvat's, mortal nature, is indicated by the fact that he is bound to a revolving wheel — a *bhava-cakra*) by a "cloud" in the "semblance" (*simulacrum*) of Juno or Hera (see citations in Cook, *Zeus* III.74f., especially *Myth. Vat.* 3.4.6 *"Ixion of Juno sought the marriage bond; she adorned a cloud in her fair form, and when Ixion joined with it, he begot the centaurs"*.

On Castor and Polydeukes (or Pollux), see Pindar N.O.X., Euripides, *Electra* 1342f, Euripides, *Helena* 690 (*leu-koppoi*) and *Aeschylus*,vol. II, p. 410 (Loeb Classical Library); also *Homeric Hymns*, 33 on Dioscuroi.

Now it can hardly be doubted that all these births of different mothers, one immortal and the other a likeness or transformation of the first, are really the divine and human births that are predicated in various ways of every solar hero, e.g. Heracles, Agni, Buddha, Mahāvīra, Christ; of whom Heracles, son of Zeus by Alcmene, was made a legitimate son of Juno; Agni is *dvimātā* (ṚV *passim*); Buddha was born of Māyā who had been made "in the likeness of the other" (*Lalitavistara*, Lefmann p. 27, 1.12), i.e. born of "Māyā the daughter of Māyā" (AV VIII.9.5), i.e. of Aditi (Mother Earth) daughter of Aditi (mother of gods), ṚV VIII.55.2, and it is to be noted that Māyā "like every mother of a *bodhisattva*" died early, that is, deserted the child, who was fostered by Pajāpati; Mahāvīra, conceived by a *bamhaṇī* was born of a *khattiyāṇī*; while, as Eckhart says of Christ, "his birth of Mary ghostly was more pleasing to him than his birth of Mary in the flesh". It will be observed that the temporal and eternal mothers are generally named alike, or in any case are alike. It is then in agreement with an established pattern that Saraṇyū, the daughter of Tvaṣṭṛ and to be identified with Sūryā, and her counterpart or transformation, are represented to be the immortal mother of gods (Yama-Yamī) and the mortal mother of the Aśvins (who were "not originally" gods) and of "Man".

Considered from this point of view the births of Yama (Yama-Yamī) and that of the Aśvins, who are respectively Sky and Earth *ab intra* and Sky and Earth *ab extra,* are not really, but only logically, two different births.

The whole story of Vivasvat and Saraṇyū is thus only a specialized variant of that of the Spiritual Person (*ātman, puruṣa*) whose "two halves" (*pati-patnī*) are to be equated with Yama-Yamī = Agni and Earth in ŚB VII.2.1.10, and with the Egyptian Zodiacal "Twins" who are of opposite sex and are called the "two halves" of the one solar deity (Budge, loc. cit.), of which two halves the "wife" after giving birth to "Men" (*manuṣyāḥ,* patronymic of Manu and thus "the children of men") reflects that "He produced me from himself, forsooth" (*mātmana eva janayitvā,* i.e. "I am his daughter"), conceals herself (cf. *Cypria* 8, where Nemesis "dislikes to lie in love with her father Zeus" and flies from him, assuming forms of fish and animals; and Heracleitus Aph. X, "nature loves to hide"), *and becomes a cow, a mare, "and so on down to the ants", the Spiritual Person (*ātman, puruṣa*) — whom she cannot elude — assuming corresponding forms and engendering corresponding off spring (BU I.4.1.4). The theme survives in folklore in ballads of the type of "The Twa Magicians" (Child, *English and Scottish Popular Ballads,* Boston, 1904, no. 44) in which there occur such lines as "Then she became a duck. And he became a rose-kaimed drake", and there can be no doubt that the "two magicians" are ultimately the Māyinī (Sky and Earth, *māyin* and *māyā*) who couple and bring forth the Babe (Agni) in R̥V X.5.3, and equally the Māyinī Nāsatyau (Aśvins) who are Agni's kindlers in R̥V X.24.4.5, cited above.

It will follow from all that has been said above that ŚB IV.1.5.16 is essentially correct in saying that the "Aśvins are manifestly (or exoterically, *ab extra*) Sky and Earth". See TS V.6.4.1 "The Aśvins are these two" and ŚB XII.9.1.12 "these two men that seem to be in the eyes pertain to the Aśvins". If Yāska in turn explains them in more than one way, as Sky and Earth, Sun and Moon, Day and Night, or as Two Good Kings (*Nirukta* XII.1, cf. XII.10 and BD VII.126), this by no means implies, what Macdonell suggested, that "even

* Hence, as Meister Eckhart says, "to find nature as she is in herself, all her forms must be shattered". An imitation of natural forms is not an "imitation of Nature" — *parokṣa-priyā iva hi devāḥ.*

the oldest commentators were puzzled" as to what the Aśvins were (Aśvins+space" and *hearing,* see TS V.6.4); on the contrary, the alternatives are valid examples of the "conjugal names" by which, as we have seen, the Aśvins can be "explained". If we too cannot distinguish sharply between the three pairs of conjoint principles that are born of the Sun and Saraṇyū, *gandharva* and *apsaras*, whether as reality or shadow, this is not because we are "puzzled" but because the distinction between the twins *in divinis,* the cosmic twins, and the parts of the human syzygy is one of nature and not of essence. All these pairs are types of the Sacerdotium and the Regnum.

40. Cf. ŚB X.4.1.5. Agni and Indra, Sacerdotium and Regnum speaking, *ekaṁ rūpam ubhāv asāva,* "let us twain become of one form" (with a view to procreation), cf. our "be made one flesh". *Śaṁbhū,* like *eko bhū* is to be unified"; hence both expressions have a marital significance, but can also mean to "die", marriage implying the *trans*-formation of the second party, by assimilation.

41. The word *virāj* (from *rāj,* to "shine" and "rule", metaphysically coincident motions) is analogous to *vibhāsa,* "shining forth" and to *śrī* "diffusing radiance"; any such shining being necessarily also a *vibhava,* i.e. an extension of being in various directions, and thus "omnipresence", whence also *vibhūti* as "power" (cf. *exeimi,* "proceed" and *exousia,* "authority"; see also p. 10, n. 30, p. 69 and *A New Approach to the Vedas,* p. 32). Furthermore, "light is the progenitive power" (TS VII.1.1.1 and ŚB VIII.7.1.16), cf. Witelo, *Libri de intelligentis,* IX, "The light is in each living thing the origin of its movement and life". There can be no wonder that it is said of the Virāj (to be equated with Śrī and Greek *Hekatos* meaning "far-shooting", certainly with reference to "shafts of light") that "the Virāj is this Earth and he who gets the most thereof becomes the chief (*ṣreṣṭhaḥ,* also "most glorious", ŚB XII.6.1.40), cf. AB VII.15 "behold the Sun's Fortune" (*sūryasya paśya śremānam*). *She* is "the kingdom, the power and the glory" by which a ruler rules. (On Virāj see Manu I.32-33 — *tasyāṁ sa virājamasṛjat prabhuḥ*). Virāj, then, as Śrī, is identified with Indrāṇī "the Person in the left eye", Indra being the Person in the right eye (BU IV.2.3 and CU IV.15, etc.) That in ŚB III.1.3.11, 14 Śuṣṇa or Vṛtra are the Person in the eye is to be understood in connection with the fact that Indra is now what Vṛtra was (ŚB 1.6.3.1.7). For the person in the eye, see n. 101,

and also Plato *Alcibiades* I.133 and Philo, I.15. Further JUB I.43.10 Person in the eye, Indra, Prajāpati; and in Rūmī, *Mathnawī* I.1679 where "The real Man is nothing but the 'little man' in the pupil of the eye", i.e. II.100f "my own image in thine Eye", and II.444 "make the child of your eye weep over your body". Their place of union is the heart (ib., and ŚB X.5.2.11), and it is there in the heart (whether in our own heart or at the heart and capital of the external kingdom) in "sleep", i.e. the restraint of the sense powers, which are thus "possessed" (as a king possesses his Fortune) that one becomes as it were a Great King and mover-at-will in his own realm (BU II.1.17-18, cf. BG V.13).

In our context, to which the text of AV VIII.9.10 "who knoweth her progenitive-duality (*mithunatvam*)?" is so pertinent, cf. AV II.36.3 where the wife "should rule" (*vi rājatu*) her house, the Virāj is evidently (like Śrī) rather feminine than masculine, and corresponds to the Virāj of AV VIII.9 and 10 where she is at once "This" (Earth, World) and that Nature (*natura naturans*) from whom all things milk their specific qualities.

In TS V.5.4.1 Sky and Earth are respectively the *svarāj* and the *virāj* (cf. CU VII.25.2 *svarāj* and *anyarāj*), approximately Empire or Autocracy and "Vice-royalty" or "Kingship"; and it is, of course just in this sense that the supremacy of the *brahma* is related to that of the *kṣatra*.

Our text may also contain an allusion to the Virāj which is the nourishment (*anna*) produced by the Sacrifice (JB I.233.234, cf. II.82); and the probability of this is increased by the fact that JB I.233 speaks of an excess of the Yajña over the Virāj as a fault, the phrase *virān nātiyaṣṭavya* suggesting the *tāṁ sambhavann atyaricyata* of JUB I.54.7 where it is evident that it is only when this unconformity has been corrected that they became the Virāj". Virāj is Mitra's, Svarāj is Varuṇa's, BD VIII.107.

42. i.e. "He has been born as my son"; whereas in BU I.4.4 "He has begotten me of himself, i.e. "I am his daughter", cf. n. 39. Both are correct propositions, and both serve as the ground for the mother's withdrawal. The rebirth of the father as the son is in accordance with the Indian and universal doctrine of progenitive reincarnation and consequent consubstantiality of father and son; the wife who bears a son becoming thereby the husband's "second mother" (*jananī punaḥ*, AB VII.13, cf. Mbh I.68.47 [Poona edn.]).

43. Eckhart I.378, Pfeiffer 528 — Der vater gebar sīnen sun in der gotheit mit allen dinge = The father begat his son into his Godhead with all things.

44. Cf. BU I.5.12 — From the union of the Sun and the Sky emanated the vital force, *prāṇa*. It is Indra.

45. We have already (n. 5) called attention to the assimilation of Mitra to Manas and of Varuṇa to Urvaśī in R̥V VII.33.11 where the designation of Vasiṣṭha as "the son of Mitra and Varuṇa" (*maitrāvaruṇa*) can only mean that a *mithunam* of Mitra and Varuṇa has taken place, as in PB XXV.10,10, or in other words that Urvaśī, thus *manasā abhigatā*, is Vāc. In PB VII.8.1 it is equally clear that the birth of Vāma (*vāma* = *prāṇa* BU I.5.12) "amongst the gods", i.e. the birth of Vāmadeva (the *r̥ṣi* of R̥V IV.1.40), implies that a conjugation of Mitrāvaruṇau has taken place, which indeed explains the special connection of the Vāmadevya Sāman (Br̥had Uktha) with sexual intercourse (*vāmadevyam mithune protam*, CU II.13.2); cf. BU IV.1.6 where Brahma as Manas betakes himself to "the woman", i.e. Vāc, and a son like himself is born of her, as also in PB VII.6 where the father is Prajāpati; all these are versions of one and the same Urmythos.

46. From Muṇḍ. Up. III.1.3, MU VI.18, ŚB XII.9.1.17 and PB XXV.10.10, *brahmayoni* is the same as *varuṇayoni*, as Varuṇa is equated to Brahma in R̥V VIII.41.8 and MU VII.11.

47. As implied by the Anukramaṇī to AV VII.21, *mantroktātmadevatyam*, the Sun is here the Universal Spirit (*ātmā jágatas tasthúṣaś ca*) of R̥V I.115.1, the Herdsman of R̥V VII.60.2 (*sūryo . . . víśvasya sthātúr jágataś ca gopá*, cf. n. 34), the Universal Lord and Husband (*īśānaṁ jágatas tasthúṣas pátim*, Sāyaṇa *svāminam*) of R̥V I.89.5, the "multiple one" (*viśvam ékam*) who "plays the man" (*patyate*, Sāyaṇa *abhigacchati*, cf. Mitra, *brahma*, as *abhigantr̥* in ŚB IV.1.4.1) to all that is in motion or at rest (*éjad dhruvám*, R̥V III.54.8), and Parjanya of R̥V VII.101.6: in other words, the divine Eros, Gandharva, Brahma to whom the whole creation is feminine, for "All of us are the wives of one Lord, it is for Him that we shall adorn ourselves" (*haṁ sab nārī eka bhatāra, sab koi tan karai siṅgāra* — Kabir); just as considered individually the body is "the sensitive image, daughter and bride" of the soul (V. da S. Pinto, *Peter Sterry, Puritan and Platonist*, pp. 166-67). See also n. 70.

48. The two worlds (*imau lokau, dyāvāpṛthivī, rodasī, kṣāmā*, etc.), celestial and terrestrial, essential and natural, were originally one, as is often explicit and still more often implied by their "separation". This separation from one another, which is in order that there may be "room" for a procedure from potentiality to act (TS V.I.5.8, ŚB I.4.1.22-23) is variously brought about: but that the worlds are separated by the birth of the Sun, by Agni, Indrāgnī, Light or Lightning, the *axis mundi* (*skambha*) or the bridge (*setu*), "by Varuṇa's operation" or "at the fiat of the imperishable" (*akṣara*), or at Dawn, are only different ways of saying the same thing.

    Their fear or shyness of one another is generally connected with the incest motif, presupposed by the fact of their common origin, which makes them father and daughter and brother and sister, like Zeus and Hera: where there is "no duality" (*advaita*), it is only with his *own* nature that the deity *can* be united, and this could be avoided only at the price of dualism. It is, indeed, inasmuch as essence and nature are one *in divinis* that the act of creation has sometimes been thought of as auto-erotic, cf. Orpheus in *Argonautica* I.494.

    In addition to our observation in n. 42, we remark that the Theotokos is necessarily feminine to God in every possible relation, as daughter, sister, mother and bride; and to note the Christian doctrine as resumed in Dante's "O Virgin Mother, daughter of thy Son" (*Paradiso* XXXIII.I) and "Bride of the Emperor of Heaven, and not bride alone but sister and most beloved daughter . . . existing in him in true and perfect fashion as if eternally wedded to him" (*Convito*, III.12); that is to say, in the same way that Prajāpati, the Progenitor, "had Vāc alone as his own", whom he only separated from himself as a mother of whom to be born (PB VII.6; XX.14).

    In ancient Roman Law the wife was said to stand to the husband *in filiae loco*.

49. Vāc (Latin *vox*) as Theotokos is not here the Logos (Lat. *verbum*), but the means or organ by which the Logos (*bṛhad uktha*) is uttered.

    The solar Prajāpati's own child-bearing precedes and must not be confused with the giving *birth* to the child by his consort. The normal doctrine about generation applies *in divinis* as much as in the world: it is that the father of all "bears himself in himself" (*ātmany evātmānam bibharti*), and "when he pours it into the woman as seed (*tad yadā striyāṁ siñcati*) then he propagates it" (*athainaj janayati*) and her giving birth to it follows (AA II.5). In PB VII.6.1, X.3.1, XIII.11.18 and ŚB II.5.1.3, accordingly, Prajāpati sees that the embryo is within him (*garbho . . . antarhitaḥ,* cf. ṚV III.57.3 *garbham asmin,* with reference to Agni as embryo) and then separates Vāc from himself as a mother of whom to be born; just as also in ŚB VI.1.2.2, 6-11 he is specifically "pregnant" (*garbho antar āsīt . . . garbhy abhavat*) and then uniting with Vāc "expresses", *sṛjati*) those beings that he has conceived and of which she is to be the mother.

The same principles apply to the "second birth" in *upanayana,* where the spiritual father makes the disciple "an embryo within him (*garbham antas*) and bears him in his belly (*udare bibharti*) for three nights", after which he is born of Sāvitrī as his mother (*ācārya* as *Agni,* see ŚB XI.5.4.12, AV XI.5.3 and Manu II.38, 170; also Hermes Trismegistus, *Libellus* XIII.2).

That both parents are thus thought of as child-bearing, i.e. "carrying", so that we can speak of them as "two wombs, one union" (*te dve yonī, ekam mithunam,* no more contradicts their sexual and functional differentiation (one only gives birth) than does the designation of the universal parents as *pitarā* or *mātarā* in ṚV *passim* imply that both are male or both female (their Supreme Identity, *tad ekam,* is of course androgynous), or than does the couvade (of which the father's child-bearing, as explained above is certainly the mythical basis) imply any distinctive femininity on the father's part, but rather that like the *brahma,* that is both the *brahma* and the *kṣatra,* he is thought of still as a first principle in which both natures are combined.

50. R. Eisler, "Jahres Hochzeit mit der Sonne", *Orientalische Studien* (*Mitth. der Vorderasiatischen Gesellschaft,* pub. Fritz Heramel, II, 1918 pp. 21-70).

51. That the Bṛhat (i.e. Sun or Agni) is elsewhere regularly contrasted with the Rathantara (Vāc) as Heaven (m.) with Earth (f.) is to be explained by the fact that the Bṛhat — as "unspoken Logos" — is originally "within" Prajāpati (*me 'yam antarhitaḥ* PB VII.6.2) and as much identical with himself as Vāc herself, whom Prajāpati "contemplates as silence" (*tūṣṇīm manasā dhyāyāt* PB VII.6.1) *ante principium.* Thus the Logos (Bṛhat) is related to the Voice as Theotokos — the Voice being that by which the Word is spoken — both as son to mother and as husband to wife: cf. Dante's "O Virgin Mother, daughter of thy Son".

52. It follows from all this that the familiar *mithunam* of Manas and Vāc by which a concept, originally formed in silence (PB VII.6.1) is itself incestuous and metaphysically illegitimate. The formation of a concept implies distinction of subject and object, knower and known, essence and nature; it is only when these distinctions are transcended, only when knowledge of (*avidyā*) becomes a knowledge — as (*vidyā*) in *adequatio rei et intellectus*, only when knower, knowledge and known are a single act of being, that knowledge can be spoken of as "pure" — "then the intellect, having attained to the form of truth, does not think, but perfectly contemplates the truth" (St. Thomas Aquinas, *Sum. Theol.* I.34.I ad 2). "But in no way can sense know this" (ibid., I.16.3). Hence the expression "Silence is golden", where silence should be understood to mean not merely not speaking, but not thinking.

53. Cf. my "Tantric Doctrine of Divine Biunity", *Annals of the Bhandarkar Oriental Research Institute,* vol. XIX, 1938, pp. 173-83.

54. ŚB VI.1.2.4 "By means of the Sun he entered into union with the Sky"; and ŚB IX.3.1.3 "The Sky is the All, and Āditya (the Sun) is its man", also BU I.5.12 of n. 44.

55. *Śáśvatī* in Grassmann's sense 2. The designation of the Domains (Three Worlds) as "Everlasting Dawns" (*śáśvatīḥ*) corresponds to that of the "Three Realms of Light" as "indestructible" (*dūṇḍśā*) in R̥V III.56.8.

56. In full agreement with the Saṁhitā texts cited above, BD I.71-73 explains that the "Three World-Overlords" (*lokādhipatayaḥ*) are not a plurality of principles but are distinguished only by their functions; there are not three distinct deities, but only "severally named in accordance with their spheres": "they arise from one another (*anyonyayonitāḥ*), all their 'participation' is in the Spirit" (*teṣām ātmaiva tat sarvaṁ yad yad bhaktiḥ*). This last is clearly an allusion to PB XX.15.2, where the "participations" or "shares" of the three *gandharva*s are the Three Realms. It is with reference to these "shares" that we find in JUB I.7.2 *manasāi 'naṁ* (*pāpmānam bhrātr̥vyam*) *nirbhajet*.

For ŚB VI.I.2.1-4 Agni, Vāyu, and Āditya are the forms that Prajāpati assumes in relation to Earth, Air, and Sky. AB V.25 calls them the "house-fathers" (*gr̥hapatayaḥ*) of the Three Worlds (R̥V I.26.7 *hotr̥ gr̥hapati*); CU I.6.1-3 states the same relationships in terms of Sāman and R̥c; the former as Agni, Vāyu, Āditya resting upon Earth, Air and Sky in the same sense that in AB III.23 the one Sāman unites with the triple Ṛc. MU IV.6, the *locus classicus* in the Upaniṣads for the *via affirmativa* and *via remotionis,* expands the *brahma vai trivṛt* of JUB III.4.11 and calls Agni, Vāyu, and Āditya (identified with Brahmā, Rudra, and Viṣṇu) "the foremost forms of the immortal, incorporeal Brahma": to whichever one of these a man is attached, his fruition is of a corresponding world (cf. BG VII.23). But though one should contemplate and praise these forms of Brahma, thereby rising higher and higher in the worlds (cf. ŚB VIII.7.1.23 where the Universal Lights are stepping stones or rungs of the ladder — *samyānyaḥ* — whereby to ascend or descend in these worlds), one should finally deny them, in order to attain to the unity of the person (*puruṣa*).

The citations from the Saṁhitās amply suffice to show that these interpretations of the Vedic Trinity as a Triune Person are not the expressions of any "later" monotheistic tendency, but simple restatements of Vedic doctrine. They are, furthermore, in whole agreement with ṚV V.44.6 "It is just in accordance with his aspect that he is given names" (*yādṛ́g evá dádṛ́śe tādṛ́g ucyate*), cf. ŚB X.5.2.20 "As he is approached, even such he becomes" (*yáthā-yathopásate tád evá bhavati*).

It is evident that the "three *gandharvas*" are the "three-headed Gandharva", the "three-headed Sun", and that if three "Universal Lights" can be distinguished by the theologian, "there corresponds to all of them one single reality" (St. Thomas Aquinas, *Sum. Theol.,* I.13.4. ad 2), that of the unity of the Person, Brahmā, Savitṛ, Prajāpati, Spirit, and Light of lights (*ātman, jyotiṣāṁ jyotis, jyotir uttamam,* etc.); the Father, Mover, Pastor (*gopā, govind,* see n. 57), and emperor of all that is in motion or at rest. The customary distinction of "Hinduism" from "Brāhmanism" is essentially fallacious; it rests on nothing more than the modern historian's sense of an obligation to demonstrate an "evolution" of thought.

The Hindu Trinity of Powers consists of a solar Father above, a fiery Son on earth (whence he ascends to heaven), and the Gale of their common spiration, and is thus indistinguishable from the Christian Trinity (it also corresponds to Plato's threefold constitution of the whole soul). It is even more exactly and in detail the equivalent of the Gnostic doctrine of the Three Christs or Triple Power: "Viewing the cosmos as a tripartite unit (= *trivṛ́tam,* ṚV X.114.1) . . . they taught that the Saviour was manifested in the three divisions in a form and manner suited to the mode of being and needs of each. . . . In his capacity as μονογενὺς (*monogenes,* one in nature) he is related to the cosmos as a *whole,* while the designation Triple-Power signifies his association with the universe as triply divided" (Baynes, *Bruce Codex,* pp. 64, 77). Cf. BD I.99, 100 and BU I.2.3 on the three forms of Agni. Cf. René Guénon, *La Grande Tríade,* Chap. 17.

The Indologist's conviction of an Indian polytheism and pantheism is a residue of Christian prejudice surviving even in the rationalist. In a parallel connection Goodenough remarks:

> Philo himself was fully aware of the universal tendency in paganism toward the doctrine of a single supreme deity. In one place he says: "But if he exists whom with one accord all Greeks and barbarians acknowledge together, the Supreme Father of gods and men and the Maker of the whole universe, whose nature is invisible and hard to grasp not only by the eye but even by the mind." . . . Coulsen in his note on this passage cannot believe his eyes that Philo thus ascribes monotheism to all pagans. So far as I can see Philo was telling the simple truth as he saw it, not as Christian propaganda has ever since misrepresented it.
>
> — *An Introduction to Philo Judacus,* p. 105

It was not, however, at any rate not in India, that "the approach to this monotheism had been by the reduction of individual deities to aspects of the single divine power", as Goodenough assumes: on the contrary, it was precisely the universality of the supreme deity that made it possible for local deities to be accepted as forms of That One (*tad ekam*) who is of many aspects (*purvanīka*) and polynominal (*bhurīṇi tava* . . . nāma, ṚV III.20.3). It is only by a *wilful* disregard of Vedic dicta, an inadequate correlation of texts, and it must be added, a general ignorance of theology and of metaphysics, that any sort of plausibility can be given to the notion of a Vedic polytheism. *Ei polloi geloiotaton* (Hermes Trismegistus, *Lib.* XI.1.11)!

Cf. Plotinus, *Enneads,* IV.4.8; Dionysius, *De divinis nominibus;* St. Thotnas Aquinas, *Sum. Theol.,* I.13.3 and especially I.31.2 "We do not say *the only God,* for deity is common to several"; also my "Vedic Monotheism" in the *Journal of Indian History,* XV, 1936.

57. In the Buddhist story of the Bodhisatta Jotipāla ("Protector of the Light", D. II.220 f.) the purohitaship to which he succeeds is referred to as the *govindiya* (not in the PTS *Dictionary*), and the *purohita* is the

Mahā-Govinda (cf. *Sarva Siddhānta Saṁgraha* XII.54, *saccidānanda govinda-paramātmā*). This epithet does not mean "high treasurer" as rendered by Malalasekara, for it was not the *purohita*'s function to act as treasurer: nor does it mean "High Steward" in the special and literal sense of "Lord of the Herds" as is suggested in *Dialogues* 2.226. It much rather means "Shepherd of the Flock" or "Pastor" in that sense in which the Sun, Agni, or Bṛhaspati is the "herdsman of the World (*jagatas* or *bhuvanasya gopā*), and in that of John X.14 "I am the good shepherd and know my sheep". The pastorate of a kingdom reflects the herding of the "unfaltering herdsman" (*gopām*, ṚV I.164.31, cf. JUB III.37, I and III.29.6 AV VII.53.2, Agni: *gopā adhipā vasiṣṭhaḥ*, that of "the herdsman of the world, the knower, whose kine are never lost" (*vidvān ánaṣṭapaśur bhúvanasya gopāḥ*, ṚV X.17.3, where *vidvān gopāḥ* is just what *govit*, *govindu*, and *govinda* mean). That "his is a herdsman's tongue" (*gopājihvasya*, ṚV III.38.9) is as much as to say that the flock knows his voice and follows him (as in John X.4 and 27).

We digress to remark that the notion of a divine shepherd may well be of high antiquity, going back to the earliest pastoral times. The notion of a divine pastor and of an analogous human pastorate is one of the very many formulae common to Egyptian, Platonic and Vedic philosophy, nor is there anything in either of these forms of the Philosophia Perennis that can be called unique. There is an art of herding human beings, royal and statesmanlike (*Statesman*, 267 C); at the beginning of a new "period" (= Skr. *kalpa* or *manvantara*), and during the rule of Kronos (the father and predecessor of Zeus), "God himself was the herdsman of men, watching over them" (ibid., 271 E); "the type of the divine shepherd (*theios poimēn*) is greater than that of the king" (ibid., 275E, cf. *Republic* 440D where the brave and eager principle, the lover of victory — i.e. the kṣatriya and *jiṛṇu* part of the soul — is the ruling shepherd's "dog"). The royal art is one of "judgement and watching over" (*Statesman* 292B). In all these statements, of course, we must not be misled by the word "royal", because Plato's conception of govemment is essentially theocratic (*Laws* 713E, cf. *Republic* 431B, *Meno* 99F), and by "king" he means priest — or philosopher-king, or in any case a government by both in complete agreement (*Republic*, 473 f., cf. *Statesman* 290E). In Christianity the Good Shepherd is "both king and priest, Thy kingdom come" (Mat. VI.9): where the priesthood and the kingship move together in one accord (*yatra brahma ca kṣatraṁ ca saṁyañcau carataḥ saha*), that holy world I fain would know" (VS XX.5, cf. n. 18, p. 50). The government and care of men is preeminently the sacerdotal function, but in so far as the royal function is delegated to a king the latter can also be called a shepherd of men, as in some of the Indian texts where the king too is a *gopā*. We need hardly add that Kṛṣṇa's epithet Govinda, and that he is the "Divine Cowherd", do not mean that he was in any historical sense a herdsman by caste but that he is a solar hero, and like the *bodhisattva* a "descent of the Sun".

To return to India, Bṛhaspati is "our far-seeing herdsman and pathfinder" (*no gopāḥ pathikṛd vicakṣaṇaḥ*), ṚV II.23.6 and *gāḥ pra astau uta ca vidvān agāyat,* ṚV X.67.3), Agni "Lord authentic (*rājasi tvam pārthivasya paśupā iva tmanā,* ṚV I.144.6) of Sky and Earth and as it were their herdsman", "Thou who at birth didst look about upon the worlds, even as a lively herdsman that goeth round about his kine (ṚV VII.13.3, *devaḥ savitā trayamāṇaḥ,* VII.35.10, and Bṛhaspati as Gopati liberates cattle, X.67.8). The human *purohita* is, as we know, the embodiment and representative of this Agni-Bṛhaspati, and naturally exercises similar functions; he is the Pastor of the Flock, or "Shepherd of the Realm" (*rāṣṭragopā*); the marriage of the king to the priest is the "restoration (*punardāya*) of the brāhmaṇa's wife", and it is when this restitution has been made that "then the kṣatriya's realm is warded" (*rāṣṭraṁ gupitam kṣatriyasya,* ṚV X.109.3). On PB VI.6.1 Caland equatcs *rāṣṭraṁ* with *kṣatram.*

A brief expansion of the last remark may be useful. Sāyaṇa's explanation of ṚV X.109 (Griffith's "unintelligible fragment, and of comparatively late origin"!) is excellent. The Brahmā's (Vācaspati's) wife is Vāc. Misled (*de*-duced from her proper allegiance) by one "who can approach her only in sin" (ṚV X.71.9) the royal voice is no longer an expression of the Truth, but on the contrary subverts the whole cosmic order. This evil is corrected when "Agni as Hotṛ takes her hand and leads her" (*hastagṛhyā ninĀya,* i.e. marries her — in the person of the king). It is precisely this *reductio regni ad sacerdotium* that is effected in the Rājasūya, in the ritual marriage of the king and the *purohita;* and it is only when this marriage has been accomplished that "the realm is guarded (*rāṣṭraṁ gupitam,* AV V.17.3), i.e. by the Brahmā as *rāṣṭragopā,* as a wife is guarded by her husband. (cf. *Apālā* (*vāc*) restored to Vṛtra-Soma, the brāhmaṇa). The reference to the "ladle" in ṚV X.109.5 is to the performance of the sacrifice in which King Soma is now co-operative (*savratā*) with Agni; the king whose open hand is as it were a sacrificial ladle (see n. 50) is no longer one of "those who do not offer the libation" (*ná sutékarāsaḥ*, R̥V X.71.9).

The marital values of *nī* and *upanī* (to "lead", and to "lead up", "reduce", or "induct") will not be overlooked: the husband is in relation to the wife the "Duke" (*nāyaka*), she is the "Duchess" (*nāyakī*). All *reductions* of effects to causes are marital reunions. The *upanayana* of a disciple by a master is an *audgrabhana* or "lifting up" and "exaltation", and we have no doubt that the traditional marriage is really an initiation of the woman, comparable to that of a *brahmacārin* by the *ācārya*, or, that both "inductions" are "mysteries"; cf. *teleō*, etc., in the related senses to "perfect", "initiate", "be married", "die", cf. n. 40. It may well be asked whether *nīti*, "leading" and *rājanīti*, "king's leading" as designations of the "Art of Government" do not contain an explicit reference to the discipular and marital relation of the king to the *purohita*, his *guru*. In our hymn, R̥V X.109.4b and 5a the reunion of the *kṣatra* and *brahma* is expressly assimilated to the *upanayana* of a *brahmacārin* by an *ācārya*, and this is in agreement with the disciple to master relationship of the king to the priest explicit in the *Arthaśāstra* (see n. 31). We know already that the king's marriage to the brāhmaṇa is part of a sacrificial rite and involves an initiation (*dīkṣā*).

Now the induction of the disciple by the master is also an affiliation by which the former is made directly a foster-son of the master and his wife and by analogy a foster-son of God and his consort. "The mother is Sāvitrī, the *ācārya* the father" (Manu, II.170, 171, cf. AV XI.5.3). The parallel may be noted in Hermes Trismegistus, *Lib.* XIII where "the mother is Sophia . . . the will of God the inseminator . . . some man who is a son of God the mediator in this palingenesis". The master (*ācārya*) is a brāhmaṇa, that is to say a "son of Brahmā", "son of God" (as the patronymic brāhmaṇa states) and represents Savitr̥, the *brahma;* in the same way the master's wife is the representative of Sāvitrī, Vāc, as *brahmajāyā*, "the brāhmaṇa's wife" in our hymn. The pupil becomes a member of their household, in which he is fostered. In this connection it may be observed that there can be little doubt that the ancient European custom of "fostering" (of which our "boarding schools" are a late secular survival or superstition) originally involved an initiation. If marriage is also an affliation we can see why it is that the wife has been traditionally said to stand to her husband, who is also her *guru, in loco filiae,* originally a metaphysical and afterwards a legal formula; the fact of marriage making her a "daughter". These conditions are still reflected in the fact that a priest addresses the members of his flock as "my son" or "my daughter", and is himself addressed as "father", and why a nun is addressed as "mother", or "sister". And if the king's "marriage" to the brahmaṇa is strictly analogous to the induction of a disciple by a master, we can as easily see that his seduction of "the brāhmaṇa's wife" (Vāc, Sāvitrī, Sophia) in ṚV X.109 is analogous to that of a master's wife by a disciple, for which such dire penance is imposed (Manu IX.237-238, XI. 104.107).

The word *govinda* is not (as inferred by the PTS [Pali Text Society] *Dictionary* and in the *Dialogues*) the equivalent of a Sanskrit *gavendra* but, in accordance with Pāṇini (III.I.138, Vārtt. 2), of *govit,* "one who knows, or finds kine" and to be correlated with *gaveṣ,* to "wish, or seek for kine": the word division is *go-vinda,* analogous to *go-pā, go-pati* and *paśu-pā.* Moreover, *go* and *paśu,* while literally "herd", "cattle", "flock", do not by any means always mean "animals" other than men, but often refer to "man" himself, the animal man, and are thus used as the equivalent of *prajā,* "children (of men)", as in AV XIV.2.25 where the children of the bride are referred to as *paśavaḥ,* in AA II.3.2 where *paśavaḥ* denotes both animals in general and the animal man as distinguished from a "person", and in BU I.4.10 where the man who has not realized "I am Brahma", and therefore approaches some God as "another than himself, is called a *paśu,* an "animal" fitted only to be regarded as food for the gods.

58. Released from death in the Agnihotra, ŚB II.3.3.9, more fully explained in ŚB X.2.6.6.7.

59. "Dies no more" corresponds to the "O king, live for ever" of several Old Testament contexts; cf. n. 37. The present is one of the many passages (e.g. ŚB II.3.3.9) in which the connection of *punar-mṛtyu,* "recurrent death", is not with a future but with his present life. The particular context is paralleled by that of ŚB V.4.1.1 where "He who performs the Rājasūya escapes all death (*sárvān . . . mṛtyān átimucyate*), all assaults (*sárvān badhān*), only old age is his death" (*tasya jaraiva mṛtyur bhavati*); cf. n. 37. The deaths referred to are the same as the *sarve mṛtyavaḥ* (Caland, "Todesarten, Lebensgefahren", cf. *Iliad,* XII.322, "the myriads of fates of death that beset us") of JB

II.419, where they are to be avoided by "not deviating from the divine marriage, the sacrifice, etc". (*daivyāt sma vivāhān meta . . . yajñāt sma meta*). Thus one who is forearmed by initiation and sacrifice may be called "undying" (*amṛta*) "even though he has no hope of never dying at all" (ŚB II.2.2.14), a hope that he could not have, because "no one becomes immortal in the flesh" (ŚB X.4.3.9). Cf. A IV.320 — "peril of dying ever present"; and TS V.6.3.1 "wherever death is born, thence he removes it by sacrifice; accordingly the piler of the Fire lives out his whole life".

Where we speak nowadays of "surviving a mortal danger" the traditional philosophy sees an actual death and rebirth; thus in TS II.3.5.3 it is with the words "His birth is renewed again and again" (ṚV X.85.19 *navo navo bhavati jāyamānaḥ*) that the life (*āyuṣ*) of the sick man is restored (cf. St. Paul on the "inner" and "outer" man). All life, as a "becoming" (*bhava, genesis* and *otrochos tēs geneseōs*), involves the repeated death of what has been and birth of what is: reincarnation (in this legitimate sense of the word) belonging as much to this present life as to any other form of temporal existence. The application of the words "sure is the death of what has been born, and sure the birth of what has died" (BG II.27, and the basis of Socrates' argument for the survival of the soul, in *Phaedo*) is as much to daily living as to the special cases of rebirth from a mother, initiatory palingenesis, and "death when the time comes". Living (*ex*-istence, *esse*) is a repeated resurrection; life eternal has neither rebirth nor recurrent death, because it is not a becoming, but an immutable being (*essentia*). Cf. Plato, Euthydemus — All change is a dying".

In all this there is nothing peculiarly Indian. The "immortality", or rather "not-dying", envisaged by the Indian texts in which it means "living out the whole of one's life" (*manuṣyasyāmṛtatvaṁ yat sarvam āyur eti*, ŚB IX.5.1.10; *agnihotra* gives full life, ŚB XII.4.2.7; and a hundred years tantamount to *amṛtam, anantam, aparimitam*, ŚB I.9.3.18, X.I.5.4); and this is to be distinguished from an "incorruptible immortality in the world of heavenly light" (*amṛtatvam akṣitiṁ svarge loke*, KB XIII.9 and XIV.4) — the two are analogous but not to be confused — is exactly the same as the "immortality" (not-dying) described to Socrates in the *Symposium* 207 D-208 B (also in *Phaedo* 87 D as in BG XV.7-11 and Eckhart): "The mortal nature ever seeks, as best it can, to be immortal. In one way only can it succeed, and that is by becoming or generation (*genesis* — a term which may be intended to cover both ordinary "becoming", and also "progenitive reincarnation"; both involve a kind of "never dying"); since so it can always leave over a new creature in place of the old. . . . Every mortal thing is preserved in this way; not by keeping it exactly the same for ever, like the divine, but by replacing what absconds or is inveterated with something else new in the semblance of the original. Through this device, Socrates (*Theatetus* 155t), a mortal thing partakes of immortality, both in the body and in all other respects; by no other means can it be done". Similarly Plutarch, *Moralia*, 302D. This also represents the Buddhist conception of living: a repeated dissolution as one thing followed by reappearance as another (*taṁ rattiyā divasassa ca aññad eva upajjati aññaṁ nirujjhati*, S. II.96), thus overcoming recurrent death as in ŚB II.3.3.9 cited above and in JB I.13 (cf. I.5) *punarmṛtyū atimucyate yad ahorātre*, "he escapes recurrent death in that he (sacrifices) night and morning". The idea of a "participation" in immortality occurs already in ṚV I.164.21. It is the same as that of the participation of existence in being, and that of the participation of the beautiful in beauty.

Thus, that the King is made "undying" is not merely a rhetorical and flattering expression, but has a meaning; it does not mean that he will never die, but that he will not die prematurely.

60. Prayer to Agni: light for brāhmaṇas, kings, vaiśyas and śūdras — ŚB VII.4.2.21, IX.4.2.14.

61. The Vāstoṣpati, equated to Rudra (TS III.4.10.3), who is *vratapā* and associated with the *brahma* in ṚV X.61.7 is evidently the Indra of ṚV VIII.97.10: and the same as the *kṣetrasya pati* of ṚV X.66.13, VII.35.10 and IV.57.3. The Vāstoṣpati of ṚV VII.54.1 and 55.1 may be Soma (though Sāyaṇa equates *indu* in ṚV VIII. 69.1 with Indra), but even so still represents the *kṣatra*.

62. As was pointed out by Weber, *Indische Studien* V.216 the formula *Ego sum Gaius, tues Gaia* [I am Gaius (masculine), you are Gaia (feminine)] was employed in ancient Roman usage (Cicero, *Murena* 12 fin. mentions the custom).

Valerius Maximus, *De praenominibus*, has: *Ferunt enim Gaiam Caeciliam, Tarquini Prisci regis uxorem, optimam lanificam fuisse et ideo institutum, ut novae nuptae ante januam interrogatae quaenam vocarentur Gaias esse se dicerent*. Cf. Plutarch, *Quaestiones Romanae*, XXX, and the note in the edition by H.T. Rose, Oxford, 1924.

Valerius Maximus, *Concerning First Names,* has: They proposed that Caecilia Gaia, the wife of the King Priscius Tarquinius, was the best spinner, and thus it was established that new brides were asked before the door, "what are you called?", and they should say that they are Gaia, cf. Plutarch, *Roman Questions,* XXX, and the note in the edition by H.T. Rose, Oxford, 1924.

63. For references to all the parallel versions and variants see Whitney in *HOS,* XIV.766-67.

64. If we compare this with the archetypal marriage of Sūryā (to whom the human bride is always assimilated) to Soma, we find that at her marriage "the 'potentiality' (*kṛtyā,* spell, enchantment, etc.) that clings to her is removed; her relations prosper; her husband is secured by obligations. "Cast away the soiled garment, give largesse unto brāhmaṇas" — for this "potentiality" hath gotten feet (*padvatī bhūtvī*) and as a wife attends her husband".

    It is clear from this "gotten feet" that the bride's "potential" form is thought of.

    Facere = *Sacra facere* when, and only when the act of king is referred to its paradigm *in divinis,* "the act of fecundation latent in eternity". *"Thy will be done on Earth as it is in Heaven. . . . Heaven and Earth* shall be in those days as *Husband* and *Wife,* tho' one *Principle, Nature and Shape;* yet two Sexes, one the Image of the *other*: and *two Persons,* each having the *entire Principle, Nature,* and *Shape, Distinctly,* and *Compleatly* in itself". Peter Sterry in Vivian da Sola Pinto, *Peter Sterry, Puritan and Platonist,* 1934, p. 200.

65. *Sa* being masculine, we follow Keith in rendering *ama* and *sa* by "That" and "This" (which are often the terms in which Heaven and Earth are referred to). The marriage formula (see above, and n. 63) elsewhere has *sā,* "She", and it may be that, as Keith suggests, *sa* is an error for *sā:* we are inclined, however, to think that the masculine *sa* is the result of an attraction to the actual and obvious sex of the person addressed, for we must not overlook that the marriage formula is here applied to the case of two persons both of whom are empirically male, and that the words are spoken here only "as if" by a man to a woman. For *sā+tama* see AB III.23 and JUB I.53.

    Sky (*dyaus*) and Harmony or Music (*sāman*) are always masculine to Earth (*pṛthivī*) and Words (*ṛc*). In ŚB IV.6.7.11 for example, "There in the *sadas* that male, the Sāma, approaches that female, the Ṛc" (*tad va etad vṛṣā sama yośāṁ ṛcaṁ sadasy ādhyeti*), the reference being to the congress of Manas (grammatically n., but explicitly male in ŚB I.4.4.3 and always male to Vāc, cf. BU IV.1.6 where "the woman" is Vāc) and Vāc (always both grammatically and effectively f.): in ŚB VIII.1.3.5 the Sāman is the husband (*pati*) of the Ṛc, which is as much as to say that *ṛcaspati* = *vācaspati*. In the syzygy *vāgmanas*, *prāṇa* may take the place of *manas*, as in JU III.359, where *prāṇa* (*satya*) and *vāc* (*ṛta*) are referred to as "He" and "She" (*sa*, *sā*) and are united (*ekam abhavam*, are married); or it may with the Brahma that Vāc is conscient (BU II.2.3). It will be seen, accordingly, that grammatical gender is by no means always a final clue to the effective gender of the referents: *sāman*, *manas*, and *brahma* are grammatically neuter, but as persons effectively masculine; while conversely in JUB I.53.2 "She" has to be rendered by *yad* (n.), *sa* (m.) and *sā* (f.) to agree with *asat*, *apānaḥ*, and *vāc* (*ā+ṛ* = *aṛ*). Cf. also the discussion of gender by Keith, *Aitareya Āraṇyaka*, pp. 208-09, n. 1.

"Comparison may also be made with ŚB IV.3.2.3-4 where the cantor (*udgātṛ*) is male to the reciter (*hotṛ*, in the restricted sense) and the recitative is their offspring, AB II.5 where the vocal priest is by implication feminine to the Maitrāvaruṇa (Vāsiṣṭha, Brahmā), and AB VI.3 where naturally male persons (the Subrahmaṇya and Neṣṭṛ priests) are treated as ritually female in accordance with their symbolic functions, and the question is asked: "How is it that they consider him who is really male as if he were a female!" (*kasmād enaṁ pumāṅsaṁ santaṁ strim ivācakṣata*). The answer to this question in our context would be that it is by their respective functions that the "sex" of the Sacerdotium and the Regnum is determined. On "Sex" see also Philo, *De Fuga et Inventione* 51.2.

Every student of Indian ritual will have remarked the constant attribution of opposite sex even to inanimate objects that are made use of: an effect can only be produced by the conjunction of two functionally contrasted causes, respectively formal and material, i.e. masculine and feminine. It is for the same reasons that the initiations, rites, sacrifices, and arts that have to do with the communion of men with gods are spoken of by Plato as *erotica*. It is, in fact, so in all making by art, where the word "concept" (formulation, expression) still implies that a "conjugation" (yoking, or marriage) of intellect (*manas*) with its organ (*vāc*) has taken place. We too still speak, although quite "superstitiously" (a "superstition" is a "survival"), of a "wedding" of words to music. In Western coronation rites the Bishop places a ring on the king's marriage finger, an action that says as plainly as if in words, "With this ring I thee wed". Cf. Philo, *De Fuga* 150 for the significance of "Ring".

Close American Indian parallels can be cited. Thus, "in Navajo literature and art all things go in pairs, male and female sometimes, but often two of the same sex, one strong, the other weaker . . . one of the Twins is a weak aid to the other . . . Moon is the weaker of the Sun–Moon pair" (Newcomb and Reichard, *Sand-paintings of the Navajo Shooting Chant*, 1937, p. 55 and Matthes, *The Night Chant, Memoirs of the American Museum of Natural History*, vol. VI, p. 6, for example, Nature is masculine and Soul is feminine); and with reference to the necessity of such pairings is "the confirmed Navajo belief that neither sex is self-sufficient, but both are necessary to fulfilment of any sort. There are many cases where two beings of the same kind [i.e. same ostensible sex] are paired, yet they are both males and [i.e. or both] females. Holy man (Monster Slayer) and Holy Boy (Child of the Waters); Sun and Moon . . . Holy Women and Holy Girl are pairs of this kind. These combinations seem to point to the emphasis that weaker, more gentle powers are as necessary to well-being as the stronger more forceful ones. This explanation is a religious one in the light of the Navajo effort to secure harmony. . . . Blue and black are 'males' or better 'dominating' colours in the Shooting Chant, white and yellow are the 'female' or 'submissive colours'." (Reichard, *Navajo Medicine Man*, 1939, p. 78)

66. Here, and in the marriage formula of AV XIV.2.71, we render *sāman* "chant", by "harmony" (attunement or music), because "all chanting and singing is music" (AA II.3.6 *sāmātho ya kaś ca geṣṇaḥ saḥ svaraḥ*, cf. CU I.6.8 *tasya ṛk ca sāma ca geṣṇau*). *Svara* "note", "tone", or "music" is often rendered by "accent", but what is meant is really "tone" as in Chinese and early Greek, not "stress" as in English: stress is, in fact, not a poetical but a prosaic quality. The contrast of *sāman* and *ṛc* is that of a harmony that transcends speech, and a verbal articulation on which the music is supported as if in a vehicle (*vāc* as *rathantara*, PB VII.6.3.4 and 7.13-14). The Music is sung on words (*ṛcí sāma gīyate*, ŚB VIII.1.3.3) and borne or supported (*adhyūḍham*, CU I.6.1-5, *pratiṣṭhitam* CU I.8.7) on them as an earth; this relation of the Music to the Words being the same as that of the Sun to the Moon in AV XV.15.4.5, where the former is *praūḍhaḥ* and

the latter *abhyùḍhaḥ*; in these words *vaḥ* has its marital significance, and it may be noted that *prauḍhā* can be applied to a woman only when she is a virago, a relatively masculine type. Thus the harmony wedded to the Words is incarnated as if by a mother (ŚB IV.3.2.3), the Ṛc is Vāc and "the Great Litany (Agni) is her supreme adaptation" (*paramo vikāraḥ*, AA II.3.6). It is in the same way that the king brings forth (enacts) what the priest knows (cf. nn. 22, 26), and that the formation of a concept begotten by Manas or Brahma on Vāc is a vital operation (BU II.2.3, IV.1.6, and Kena U. 30).

On the other hand, the words considered apart from and in opposition to the Music (*svara*) are the "evil (*pāpman*) of the Chant, and whoever seeks to take refuge in such a toneless Ṛc (*ṛoy asvarāyām*) is found out by Death" (JUB I.16.10, I.18.8; CU I.4.3). It is because the words (*ṛc*) are the physical and mortal "body" of the Music as distinguished from itself, and "the body is given over to Death to be his share, so that no one becomes immortal with the body", that Prajāpati tells the gods to approach the world of heavenly light by means of the wordless Chant (*sāmnā 'nṛcena*) and so indeed they did, "shaking off these bodies, the verbal tracks (*etāny ṛkpadānī śarirāṇi dhūnvanta*) that lay strewn (along their path) up to the Sky" (JUB I.15.3f. with ŚB X.4.3.9); this is the same as the "ascent on wings of sound" (*svarapakṣa*, JUB III.13.10) or "wings of light" (*jyotiṣpakṣa*, PB X.4.5), or "metrical wings" (*chándaḥpakṣa*, AV VIII.9.12). Thus the *devayāna* is thought of as the *via negativa* (for the "ways of excellence and remotion" see MU IV.6): "the angles have fewer ideas and use less means than men" (Eckhart); "Not what is uttered by Vāc, not what men worship here, but that by which Vāc is uttered, know only that as Brahma . . . it is the Unknown that should be remembered, methinks" (*mimāṅsyam eva te manye 'viditam*, JUB IV.18.5 and 19.1).

But while that which can be tracked pertains to our mortality (*padena ha vas punarmṛtyur anveti*), and it is just because the immortals have left their tracks *behind them* these gods, Agni, Vāyu, Āditya, Candramas are (like the Buddha) in themselves "trackless" (*na ha vā etāsāṁ devatānām padam asti*, JUB III.35.7; *apadaṁ, kena padena nessatha*? Dh. 179), yet can be followed by their traces (*padāni*, scriptural, liturgical, iconographic, and reliquary). There could, indeed, be no other "ascent after Agni" TS V.6.8.1) than by following up the road on which the tracks are strewn of those who have gone before, until these footprints end with the road itself, beyond which lies the Unknown *summum bonum* "from which words recoil" (Taitt. U. II.4). A *via affirmativa* must precede the *via negativa:* "meanings" and images must not be discarded until they are no longer meanings *to* but meanings *of* ourselves, no longer figures of others but our own, who can then no longer see them over against "ourselves". The reader must not confuse the meta-physics of scripture with the "anti-intellectualism" of the modern mob. That the music of the spheres is "pure" of any objective sense is by no means a justification of our current love of fine sounds, miscalled "love of art"; when we say: "Leave it to pure sound when the meaning's almost nothing", this has nothing to do with the unintelligibility of the solar songs, but only commends the sensitive and aesthetic art of the charmer of snakes.

It must not be gathered from what has been said above that the Chant is a music incomplete for lack of words. On the contrary, just as Agni is both Mitra and Varuṇa (ṚV VII.12.3), "the great Brahma, one *akṣara,* inexpressible Ātman, is both the *brahma* and the *kṣatra*" (ŚB X.4.1.9 with ŚA XIII), *parāpara* (MU VI.23), *niruktānirukta, śabdāśabda,* etc., and can therefore as *brahma* stand alone, which is no more possible for the *kṣatra* (ŚB IV.1.4.2-3) than for a woman (Manu V.148, cf. IX.2), and just as the spirit (*ātman*) is in itself an androgynous syzygy (BU I.4.3, cf. Plato, *Symposium,* 189E) and only by a schism of its two selves becomes a husband and wife, or *brahma* and *kṣatra,* so the quiddity of the Chant or Harmony (*sāmnaḥ sāmatva*) is explained as the biunity of its logically differentiated elements, tone (*svara*) and words (*ṛc*); the congress (*samiti, saṁdhi, mithuna,* etc.) of the masculine and feminine principles, like that of their verbal symbols (*sā+ama* = *sāman*), making up the incomposite whole of the harmony itself (a whole that had never been diminished by the differentiation of the words); it is only the mere words in themselves, and not the words as the support (*pratiṣṭhā*) of the Harmony, that are "evil"; and in the same way for the relationship of the Sacerdotium and Regnum, or Inner and Outer Man.

It has, of course, been generally overlooked that in KU II.23 where there is a "choice" of one self by the other; in BU IV.4.23 where "the pacified and dompted (*śāntó dāntáḥ*) and composed (*samahitaḥ,* 'in *samādhi*') self sees itself only in the Self" (*ātmany evātmanam paśyet,* i.e. being in the spirit sees only the Spirit, sees itself not as it is in itself but as it is in God); in BU IV.2.1 *samahitātmā* (self-composed), AA III.2.1 *prāṇe . . . samāhitaḥ,* and AA III.2.6 *ātmānaṁ samadadhāt* (Keith, "put himself together"), *samādhi* implies the *ātmamithunaḥ* of CU VII.25.2, *saṁdhā* goveming *ātmānam* always referring to the *hieros gamos* that is to be consummated within you, in the heart. In the arts, *saṁdhā* (cf. *harmoxo harmonia*) has the analogous value to "fuse" or "weld" or otherwise "fasten" together two different metals, or such incongruous materials as wood and iron (in the latter case with glue, *śleṣmaṇa,* √*śliṣ*, to "embrace", in the former by means of a "salt"), and "even so the comprehensor heals everything" (*sarvam bhiṣajyati*) by the utterances (*vyāhṛtayaḥ*) *bhūr, bhuvas, svar* (the reference of which utterances is to the unions of Agni with Earth, Vāyu with Space, and the Sun with the Sky), JUB III.17.2-3.

The grammatical *saṁdhi* and *saṁhitā* are, in fact, only a special case in the long series of analogous conjunctions discussed in ŚA VII and VIII and corresponding passages of AA, and elsewhere. In the case of all these unions the end in view is an effective harmony and the reproduction of the higher of the two principles involved. In general the junction is a combination (*saṁhitā*) of the parents in their child (ŚA VII.15, cf. Taitt. U. I.3), so that, for example, "science" (*vidyā*) is the conjunction of Intellect and Voice, Manas and Vāc, jointly necessary to the expression of any concept of truth (ŚA VII.7).

Now in the case of the macrocosmic harp (the seven-rayed Sun) and that of the analogous human instrument with its seven "breaths", AV XV.15.2, etc.), the man himself (cf. A III.374 f., where in the "figure", *nimitta,* of the harp, the right tuning of the strings to a mean that is neither too taut nor too slack corresponds to the proper adjustment of the man's force and faculties, *viriya* and *indriyāṇi:* Plato, *Rep.* 349E, 412A and *Phaedo*), the combination (*saṁhitā*) that is its "force" (*tviṣi* = *bala* in Taitt. U. I.2) is that of the skilled player with the instrument itself, these two being the formal and efficient causes of the audible harmony or euphony; we read that "Just as the harp struck by a skilled player accomplishes the last end (whole reason, *raison d'*) of the harp, so the voice impelled by a skilled speaker accomplishes the last end of the voice" (*evam eva kuśalena vaktrā vāg ārabdhā kṛtsnaṁ vāgarthaṁ sādhayati,* ŚA VIII.10. Cf. BG II.50, *yogaḥ karmasu kauśalam*), and it is certainly pertinent to the Kingship that we are told that "He who is a Comprehensor of this divine harp (the seven-rayed Sun) becomes exceedingly famous: his renown fills the earth; men hearken to him when he speaks in the assemblies, saying: "Let this be done which he desires" (ŚA VIII.9). The speaker, like the King and other artists, is thought of as a *sādhaka,* "one to hit the mark". Here then is a rhetoric of "the energising of truth, the bringing to bear of truth upon men" (Baldwin, *Mediaeval Rhetoric and Poetic,* p. 3). For it is clear that the "last end" of the musical speech is by no means one of fine sounds for their own sake (for which the voice alone, uninformed by any meaning would suffice; it has been remarked that "To exercise freedom of speech one needs only vocal cords"), not what the sense powers (*indriyāṇi*) have to offer, not amusement, but that "science without which art is nothing", that "science" (*vidyā*) for which the co-operation of Manas with Vāc, Inner Sage and Outer King, *philosophia* and *dynamis,* is required, that "meaning of the Vedas" by which, if one understands it, the *summum bonum* (*sakalaṁ bhadram*) is attainable (ŚA XIV). We need hardly say that this is also precisely Plato's (and the universal) doctrine of the purpose of art: we are endowed by the gods with vision and hearing, and harmony was given by the Muses to him that can use them intellectually (*meta nou* = *manasā*), not as an aid to irrational pleasure (*hēdonēn alogon*) as is nowadays supposed, but to assist the soul's revolution (*psiches periodon,* cf. *cittavṛtti* and *vrata*), to restore it to order and concord with itself (i.e. the "Self", the Inner Man of *Phaedrus* 279C). And because of the want of measure (*ametron*) and the lack of graces in most of us, rhythm (= *numerus, saṁkhyāna*) was also bestowed upon us by the same deities and for the same ends" (*Timaeus* 47 D, E): the composition of sounds is the basis of an affect (*pathē*) that affords, indeed "pleasure (*hēdonē*) only to the unintelligent, but to the intelligent (*emphron* connected with *phrēn* "heart", "mind" and = Skr. *sahṛdaya*) that heart's ease (*euphrosynē*) also which is induced by the mimesis of the divine harmony made manifest in mortal motions" (*ib.* 80 B, echoed in Quintilian's *docti rationem componendi intelligunt, etiam indocti voluptatem* [The learned in uniting understand reason, the unlearned understand only pleasure] IX.4.116, and in St. Augustine's deprecation of those "who enjoy what they should use"). Plato's conception of the "whole end of the voice", or more generally of the whole purpose of art (since he regards all craftsmen as "poets", *Gorgias* 503), is identical with that of the Āraṇyakas, and it is clear that his "delight", so carefully distinguished from "pleasure", is no more "aesthetic" than is the "savouring of the flavour (*rasāsvāsvādana*) that the *Sāhitya Darpaṇa* (III.2-3) speaks of as "Intellectually beatific" (*ānandacinmaya,* cf. A III.354 *paramaṁ ñānam- . . . sukham anuttaram*) and as the "twin brother" of the "savouring of Brahma"; *rasa* corresponding to the '*sap*' in *sapientia, 'cognitio cum amore'* ("understanding with love"). In the present context the application is to the art of government, likened to that of music; the end of this art is not the King's pleasure, but his "children's" and his own good. As in any other vocation (*svadharma*) the King is to be governed by his art, not "expressing himself, the instrument, but voicing what has been dictated by the intellect, *nous* (*manasā vā agre kīrtayati,* ŚA VII.2, cf. John VIII.28 and Dante, *Purgatorio,* XXIV.52.54), and making the good of the work to be done his only concem (*karmaṇy evādhikāras te,* BG II.47). In the last analysis, God is the skilled player and we the harp of which the "strings" or "senses" must be "regulated".

We begin to see now why the words (*ṛc*) should be studied (*adhīyītā,* i.e. like all other symbols, as supports of contemplation, *dhiyālamba*) in their *saṁhitā* form, that form in which they are sung, and in which alone are they "life-giving" (*āyuṣya,* ŚA VIII.11), i.e. productive of *dīrgham āyuṣ* here (the life of 100 years; "immortality" for man = 100 years of life, ŚB XIII.1.5.6 and PB XXIV.19.2) and hereafter (imperishable immortality). It is because the re-constitution (*ātmasaṁskṛti*) of the disintegrated and manifold self effected in the Sacrifice (for which the Chant is absolutely indispensable, TS II.5.8.4) is essentially metrical: "the sacrificer perfects himself as composed of the metres" (*chandomayaṁ saṁskurute,* AB VI.27, Keith's rendering), and is thus a "perfected Self" (*sukṛtātman,* Taitt.U. II.7): Prajāpati, broken up in the emanation of his children (cf. ŚB X.5.2.16 on the One and the Many) "unifies himself by means of the metres" (*chandobhir ātmānaṁ sama-dadhat,* AA III.2.6 and ŚA VIII.II), i.e. "synthesises" the manifold self with the simple Self (the rebel with the rightful sovereign). Similarly, in the *samādhi* of the Yogaśāstra where there is a reconciliation and "synthesis" of hostile, selves, and in the *samādhi* of the *Arthaśāstra* where *samādhi* or *saṁdhi-karaṇa** is the making of a treaty of peace and alliance (also explained as a

* Cf. *suśliṣṭenāpi saṁdhinā* "Even with a very close alliance" enemy is still an enemy. Edgerton, *Pañcatantra* II.105, 106, 333.

sambhāvanā, a term so often employed in connection with marital alliances) between two powers that have been at war, and the converse *samādhi-* or *saṁdhi-mokṣa* (= *saṁdhi-bheda*) is the dissolution or breaking of such a treaty and analogous to the grammatical *saṁdhivivartana* = *padaccheda,* the "divorce" of fused words; it will be seen that I cannot wholly agree with Edgerton's rendering of *samādhi* by "hostage" (see his "*Samādhi,* 'Hostage'. . . ", in *JAOS* 60.208ff.) but rather hold that the *samādhi* (synthesis) is a "treaty of peace" commonly ratified or secured by an exchange of gifts or "deposits" (*āhita*), not excluding those of persons such as a daughter given in marriage (rather as a pledge than as a hostage); the pledges or hostages are given when the peace is made, and there is nothing to show that any such hostages were held while the fighting was going on, which hostages could be "released". In any case all these "agreements" are analogous to that of the "two selves" of Mitrāvaruṇau and all those other aspects of the union of contrary principles, in which there is always an exchange of gifts, each giving something of its own to the other: all these ἐρωτικά (*erotica*) are makings of harmony and order where discord had been, and we can say with Dionysius (*De div. nom.* IV.5) that "all alliances and friendships are because of the beautiful"; this will apply, for example to the "alliance" of words in grammatical *saṁdhi,* for the metrical *saṁhitā* texts are assuredly beautiful, the mere words (*ṛc*) being the "evil" of the chant, and *kalyāṇa* the opposite of *pāpman* as is *pulcher* of *turpis.*

On the other hand, in *pada texts* the blank space (*avakāśa*) or moment of time (*mātrā*) "divorces the conjunction" (*saṁdhiṁ vivartayati,* cf. ṚV VI.9.1 *vivartete rájasî* and VII.80.1 *vivartīyantiṁ rájasī;* and *vivrata,* "contrasted operation") and divides (*vibhajati*) or distinguishes (*vijñāpayati*) the long and short syllables (*mātrāmātram*) and tonic (in Webster's sense 4 b) from "atonic" (*svarāsvaram*), AA III.1.5 with ŚA VII.12 such a formulation is certainly not meant to be understood *only* grammatically (grammar itself is a traditional "Way" and "Doctrine"; cf. CUII. 22.3-5, Tait. U. I.3.1, and Faddegon, *Studies on Pāṇini's Grammar,* 1936, pp. 67-68): the "divorce" of the metrically fused syllables is, as much as the divorce of Sky and Earth, their disaccord and discord: *mātrā* is the quantitative "matter" that fills space (*mātrā* as *materia* BU IV.3.9), and *avakāśa* (= *ākāśa, antarikṣa,* Sāyaṇa on PB XVIII.9.6) the luminous sphere that intervenes between the Earth and Sky; *mātrā* and *amātrā* can be taken to refer to what has measure or number and what has not (the distinction of poetry from prose); while the distinction of *svara* (tone, tune, music, "the gold of the chant", BU I.3.25-26) from what is *asvara* (tuneless noise) — in ŚA. I emend to *asvarāt svaram* to agree with AA *svarāsvaram* — can be equated with that of the intoned (*svarya*) chant from the toneless libretto (*ṛc*, "the evil of the chant", JUB I.16.10) and furthermore with that of solar light from mundane darkness (it can hardly be conveyed in English that *svar* implies both "tone" and "light", though we can speak of a "brilliant tone", and Dante spoke of "singing suns"). Strong confirmation of these interpretations can be found in a correlation of AA II.3.6 where we are told that "vain talk is unmeasured" (*vṛthā vāk tad amitam*) — we understand this to mean at once "unmetrical" and "immoderate" — with JB II.69, 70, 73 where in the sacrificial contest between Prajāpati and Death "what was sung or danced to the harp by way of mere entertainment" (*vṛthā* = *mógham*, "vainly", in the corresponding text of ŚB III.2.4.6) by Death is "unnumbered" (*asaṁkhyānam*) and "deadly" (*martyam*), and what by Prajāpati "numbered" (*saṁkhyānam*) and "lively" (*amṛtam*), and death's music is now our secular art of the "parlour" (*patnīśālā*), "whatever people sing to the harp, or dance or do to please themselves" (*vṛthā*): and with ŚB III.2.4.1.6 where the mundane Devas (*ihá devāḥ*) contest with the celestial (*divi*) Gandharvas for the possession of Vāc; the Gandharvas say to her: "We are declaring the Vedas, we know, indeed we know" (*vai vayáṁ vidma*, cf. ŚB XI.2.3.7), but the mundane Devas: "We will amuse thee" (*tvā pramodayiṣyāmaha*); Vāc is seduced by the sensitive Devas, "and that is why even nowadays women are wedded to folly" (*móghasaṁhitāḥ*); but finally won by the Gandharvas from them. The word *prámodayiṣyāmaha* is reflected below (16) in the expression *prakāmódya* "aesthetic, or appetitive conversation", evidently contrasting with *brahmodaya*, "godly conversation" or "Brahmanical colloquy" (see Bloomfield in *JAOS* 15.184 and Caland on PB IV.9.12): the distinction of celestial Gandharvas from the mundane Devas is the same as that of the *brahmagandharvāḥ* from the *devāḥ* in TS VI.1.6.5-6, that of the *divikṣit* from the *lokakṣit* Devas in CU II.24.14, and that of the *devas* whose spokesman is the Sacrifice from the Asuras — the unregenerate sense-powers, *prāṇāḥ, indriyāṇi* — in ŚB III.2.1.18 where also the contest is for Vāc; the mundane Devas are of those who "can only approach Vāc in sin" in the sense of ṚV X.71.9. The distinction of such an "unmodulated vain conversation" (*vṛthā vāk . . . amitam*) from the "Chant commensurate with the spiritual-Self (*ātmasammitam- . . . sāma*, CU II.10.1), "commensurate with the Imperishable" (*akṣarasammānas . . . ātmā*, SA VIII.5, i.e. with the syllable *oṁ*, with Brahma, not Keith's "letters"), is very evident. Sāyaṇa's explanation of *vṛthā vāk* in AA II.3.6 is "non-Brahmanical interpretations (i.e. "free examination"; *agata* is very literally "unauthorized", "not fathered by") and humorous anecdotes and so forth told at court or other such like places" (*brāhmaṇagatā ye 'rthavādā yā ca rājasabhādau parihāsādirupeṇocyate*).

The sacred "science of the celestial Gandharvas" (who know better than the Rṣis what is too much or too little in the Sacrifice, ŚB XI.2.3.7) and "science" (*vidyā*) of ŚA VII.15, must not be equated with our profane science, but with "metaphysics" (cf. René Guénon, "Deux sciences" in *La crise du monde moderne*, 1927, and *La metaphysique orientale*, 1939; Gaigneron, *La connaissance interdite*, 1935). An accumulation of knowledge for its own sake, to satisfy a curiosity, is as much as gossip, vaudeville, or any merely sentimental art or "art for art's sake", a "profanity" (*vṛthā vāk:* we say "profanity" here with reference to the opposition of profane to sacred (ἱερός *ieros, brahma*), Brahmā), and the fact that *vṛthā*, from √*vṛ*, to 'choose', is the semiotic equivalent of 'heretical', from *aireo* (*aireomai*) to 'choose for oneself'; the man who can boast, or even admit that "I do not know what is right, I know what I like to do; I do not know what is true, but what I like to think; and I do not know anything about art, but know what I like" is in the strictest sense of the word a "heretic", one who however "well-intentioned" is nevertheless "opinionated" and "unprincipled".

Stated in other words, there is a distinction of a significant (*padārthābhinaya*) and liberating (*vimuktida*) art — the art of those who singing here to the harp are celebrating Him, the Golden Person, in both his natures, immanent and transcendent — from an in-significant art "coloured by worldly passion" (*lokānurañjaka*) and "dependent on the moods" (*bhāvāśraya*); the former is the "highway" (*mārga*) and the latter a "pagan" (*deśī*) art (CU I.7.6-9 with *Saṁgītadarpaṇa*, I.4-6 and *Daśarūpa*, I.12.14). The distinction of *mārga* from *deśī* is not, of course, one of fine from applied or of high from folk art, but of the traditional art that follows up the main track to its destination at "World's End" from a naturalistic art that wanders off the main road "in all directions" (cf. *yathā diśam* = *yathāvaśam*); the root meanings present in *deśī* are to "display", and "all directions" (*disi diśī*, cf. *diśo diśas*, "hither and thither"). Whence *deśa* "country" or "environment", "outlandish parts" as distinguished from the "heart" of the kingdom, while *pāgus* is also "country" and "pagan", "outlandish", and thus heterdox. The "pagan" art by which we are seduced, i.e. led *off* or led *away* from the relatively "narrow" Way is essentially femininc: cf. ŚB III.2.1.22 where the Devas (Gandharvas) remark that "Vāc is a woman" (*yóṣā*), and are fearful "lest she ensnare" (*ná yuvitā*; cf. ṚV I.105.2 where Trita laments *ā jāyā yuvate patim*) the Sacrifice, her suitor on their behalf. This fear is, of course, the basis of the Indian, Islamic, and Christian "puritanism", which must not be misinterpreted to the discredit of all art and is a disparagement only of the profane arts of amusement, of mere diversion, Plato's "art of flattery". There is obviously no disparagement of the Cantor who sings of the Sun on his harp by means of the "Threefold Science" (*trayī vidyā*, i.e. *bhūr bhuvas svar*, JUB I.58.1-2; II.9.7; III.18.4), the harpists whose song is "of Him", the person in the Sun, the lord of these worlds thereunder and of men's desires, and so singing win both worlds (CU I.7.6, I.11), or of the art (*śilpa*) of dancing, singing, and instramental music referred to in KB XXIX.5; no disparagement of scripture with its "figures of thought", but only of "literature" with its "figures of speech"; none of "poetry", but only an affirmation of its real values (*artha*), a justification of such "scientific" poets as Dante who, with his *dottrina che s'asconde sotto ilvelame degli versi strani* ". . . doctrine which conceals itself beneath the veil of strange verses", *Inferno* IX.62-63 and confessed amanuensis of Eros, was no more than any Vedic *ṛṣi* or *mantrakṛt* a litterateur, but a soothsayer, *satyavādin*.

And just as there is no disparagement of art as such, so in the so-called misogynism of the texts there is no more disparagement of woman as such than there is of things as such; the disparagement is of an effeminacy to which both are liable by a perversion of their naturally and therefore properly "erotic" nature: a disparagement of monarchy, like that of the spiritual power, is an altogether modern development, essentially proletarian and "materialistic". It is not "this woman", but the feminine, or rather effeminate, principle which, *when it follows its own devices*, makes pleasure its end, is rejected, whether in woman or man, subject or king. We are all of us, like Aditi-Vāc, "double-headed" (*ubhayataḥśīrṣṇī*), having one tongue "worshipful and regal" (*kṣatriyā hy éṣā yajñiyā*) that enunciates the Guerdon (*dákṣiṇā*) of the Sacrifice, the wisdom (*vidyā*) by which the whole end of Speech, and immortality, are won; and another that perverts the Truth (ŚB III.2.4.16 with JUB IV.19.4); the latter is condemned, but not the tongue as such.

We realize now that art can have, not only "fixed ends", but also "ascertained means of operation"; that it is not only for those who sing here to sing of Him, but to sing as He sings. On the one hand, a prosaic, historical and anecdotal, sentimental and humanistic interpretation of "scripture as literature", or of any traditional symbol, whether auditory or visual, is a deadly error (cf. S. I.11), the defect of Plutarch's Greeks, who could not distinguish between Apollo and Helios, and because of which many learned Indians have thought of European scholarship as a crime. On the other it is clear that our substitution of stress for tone, our "expressive" and informal manner of reading and singing — so different from the measured "singsong" of traditionally spoken verse — are essentially profane developments characteristic of an age that can no longer think of song as an evocative or creative (*poiētikos*) art in any literal sense of the words, or of the sacrifice as necessary for our daily bread. We realize the significance of the fact that prose has been a late development in literary history; ours is a prose style, while the traditional lore of all peoples — even the substance of their practical sciences — has been everywhere poetical. The prosaic and pedestrian language of the "*pada* text" is the analytical language of fact, the intoned poetry or "incantation" the language of truth: intonation is analogous to information. It can hardly be said of *us* that our music is "an earthly representation of the music that there is in the rhythm of the ideal world" or that our "crafts such as building and carpentry take their principles from that realm and from the thinking there" (Plotinus, *Enneads,* V.9.11), or that we "make all things according to the pattern that was shown thee upon the mount" (Exodus, XXV.40), or that "our songs are the same as His songs" (CU I.7.5); for like all other animals, we know what we like; and over and above this, have invented a science of likes and dislikes — properly styled a "psychology" — and have substituted this "aesthetic" for the traditional conception of art as an "intellectual virtue". Thus when we said that *saṁdhi,* whether grammatical, erotic, or technical, was "for the sake of harmony, or euphony", this did not mean "for aesthetic reasons", for the love of fine sounds or the mere satisfaction of longings (the traditional union has other and practical ends in view, so that a man sins if he desires even his own wife "as a woman, and not because she is his wife", and it is not upon a "falling in love" but on qualifications that the marriage of king and priest depends). The point is that discord is sterile, preventing "good use", concord effective. If the texts are to be made "enchanting"(cf. Plato, *Laws* 659 E), this is not in the modern sense of the word but in that sense in which the Cantor (the Udgātṛ, assimilated to the Sun, see *JAOS* 60, 1940, p. 49, n. 12; the harpist whose songs are a mimesis of the solar music of the spheres, CU I.7.5) is strictly speaking an enchanter, voicing words of power, a chanticleer announcing the morning. If the intoned (*svarya*) text is actually also more "charming" than the prosaic reading (this time "charming" in the modern sense), this charm was not their first intention or last end; the aesthetic value of the incantation, so artfully constructed, is indeed an undeniable value, not however the value of a *raison d'être*, but that of "the pleasure that perfects the operation". A good example of the principle can be cited in the case of the lotus wreath, called a "work of art" or rather "symbol" (*śilpa*), that Prajāpati wears "for supremacy" and which he bequeathes to Indra, who thereupon becomes an all-conqueror (PB XVI.4.3-5); this wreath is assuredly an "ornament" in the word's original sense of "equipment"; it is not worn "for effect" but to be effective. Conversely, those whose language is arid (*anireṇa*, in-sapient) are thought of as unarmed (ṚV IV.5.14). Cf. my "Ornament" in *Art Bulletin*, XXI.1939.

We find it strange that, with the exception of Gonda, students of Indian rhetoric have completely neglected the older and also the Buddhist material on the "purpose of speech".

67. For *purāṇi* Sāyaṇa has *grāmāḥ*, "villages", but this does not mean, as Keith suggests in a footnote, "villages in the kingdom"; on the contrary the "villages" are those of Sky and Earth, as in CU VIII.6.2 where the two worlds are *grāmau*, "two villages", cf. ŚB X.2.5.1 where "These worlds, indeed are strongholds" (*purāḥ*). For "worlds as citadels", see AB I.23. In JUB I.53.3 the Two Worlds are *āyatanāni*; and in AB IV.27, the *purohita* the kings's *āyatana*. In TS III.4.7.3 the Two Worlds are *upari gṛha iha ca*, "the upper house and this one

here below", the latter being the *adharād gṛha* of AV II.14.3. In TS IV.2.5.1 the formula for the marriage of the two Agnis (*brahma* and *kṣatra, ib.* V.2.4.1) concludes with the words *bhavataṁ naḥ samanasau** *samokasau,* which are found also in TS I.3.7 where they are addressed to the firesticks, identified with Urvaśī and Purūravas as parents of Āyu-Agni: *samokasau,* cf. Gk. *synoikeō,* being literally "cohabitant". This reflects ṚV X.65.8 *parīkṣitā pitarā pūrva jāvarī ṛtasya yonā kṣayataḥ samokasā dyāvāpṛthivī varuṇāya savrate....* "Sky and earth cohabiting, co-operating, at the source of justice", i.e., at the sacrificial altar.

In JB I.145, where again it is a question of the "divine marriage" of the Two Worlds (cf. PB VII.10.3 and AB IV.27), the result is that now "they dwell in one another's house (*anyo 'nyasya gṛhe*) and it is as hard to see why Caland *Das Jaiminīya Brāhmaṇa in Auswahl,* p. 47) found the plural, *vasanti,* so strange as it is to see why Keith (who fails to remark the marital force of TS I.3.7 and TS IV.2.5.1) should have thought that Sāyaṇa had overlooked the marital force of the formula in AB VIII.27. What of the plural in "They twain shall be one flesh" (*Matthew* XIX.5) and Vidyāpati's "Each is both"?

There is a very significant parallel here between the Sanskrit and the Greek sources. In the first place the two words *pur* (or *pura*) "city", and *samokasa* ($\sqrt{uc}$, to "be apt for") "living in one house with" are the etymological equivalents of Greek *polis* and *synoikeō.* Both the Sanskrit and the Greek sources speak of man as a "city": for example, man's body is a "city indwelt by God" (*brahmapura,* CU VIII.1.1, Muṇḍ. Up. II.2.7. — the term also meaning "city of God", i.e. Heaven), the head is the body's *acropolis* (*Timaeus* 70A). Furthermore, just as Sky and Earth are to be "cohabitant" (*samokaś*) "here", so the divine, daimonic, immortal part of the soul is said to "live in one house with" (*synoikeō, Timaeus* 90 A, C, etc.) the mortal part of the soul: and if Plato does not expressly interpret this to mean a cohabitation of male and female principles, such a distinction is certainly latent in the fact that the two principles are for him by nature respectively the dominant and the obedient.

We can still speak of a marriage as an "alliance of two houses", and of the married pair as "cohabiting". There can be no possible doubt

---

* It is by a curious coincidence that this word *sa-manasau,* if analysed as *sam-anasau* would mean "sharing one vehicle", cf. *saṁ-vah* to "drive off together", with a view to "living together" (*saṁ-vas*).

that the *purāṇī*, "cities", Sāyaṇa's *grāmāḥ*, in our context are Sky and Earth, the city of God and the city of man.

68. The two "forms" or "bodies" (*tanū*) of the *purohita* and the king correspond to the "two forms" (*vām . . . tanūnām*) of Mitrāvaruṇau in R̥V V.67.5, and to their "two selves" or "two persons" in ŚB; IV.I.4.1. In PB VII.10.3 it is by means of their "two dear bodies" (*priye tanvau*), the *naudhasa* and *śyaita* metres, that the divine marriage (*daivam mithunam*) of Sky and Earth (*br̥hadrathaṁtarau*) is consummated, the union being effected by an exchange of verse endings. For this kind of "transposition of forms" in marriage, comparable with the *līlāhāva* of the later rhetoricians, cf. PB VII.10.3 *viparikrāmati* = JB I.145 *vyavahetām*. In AB VIII.27 a reading of *saṁvihāvahai* (for *saṁvahāvahai*) would scarcely affect the meaning: cf. Caland on *vivahāvahai* in JB I.145 (JB *in Auswahl*, pp. 46, 47). The transposition and mingling of hymns in the ritual (e.g. AB VI.28 *sūkte paryasyati, sa eva tayor vihāraḥ*) is always a comingling of contrasted forms with a view to a propagation; and there is something in the assimilation of the king and priest to one another that is quite analogous to this.

That *tanūs* in our text refers to the kings's person and *tanvam* to the *purohita*'s is paralleled in TS VI.I.1.3 (also R̥V VIII.48.9 *nas tanvaḥ soma gopāḥ*, and X.7.7 to Agni — *nastanvo 'prayucchan*) — "Thou art the body of (King) Soma, protect thou my body". Cf. ŚB XIV.3.1.9 "We will follow Thee (Sūrya) for the protection of the *kṣatra* . . . guard thou the Brāhmaṇa's body!" Just as Indra, king *in divinis*, is *vratapā*, "Fidei Defensor", and becomes the Buddha's protector from the time of the Buddha's Awakening and Enthronement onwards, so the human King is *brāhmaṇānāṁ goptā . . . dharmasya goptā*, AB VIII.17. For an exchange of bodies and names, and transvestment, cf. TS I.3.4.3 and I.5.10.1.

69. Taken alone, this seems to mean "Formula for the king's choice of the *purohita*", cf. R̥V V.50.1 "Let every mortal choose (*vurīta*) the God's, the Leader's (i.e. Savitr̥'s) fellowship", X.21.1 *agnáṁ . . . hótāraṁ tvā vr̥ṇīmahe*, and III.62.10 *váreṇyam* "choiceworthy", qualifying Savitr̥'s splendour. In any case the choice is mutual (cf. ŚB IV.1.4.5-6); each "takes" the other in the sense that "take" is used in the Christian marriage service. In R̥V X.124.4 where Agni "chooses" (*vr̥ṇānaḥ*) Indra it is, of course, to be understood that Indra also "chooses" Agni, as in TS II.5.2.3. This reciprocal relationship is

paralleled in the ambiguity of the much discussed text of KU II.23, of which the real theme is that of the sacred marriage to be effected within you (cf. BU IV.3.21). In KU II.23. It is a matter of the "taking" (√*labh*, which has also an erotic sense) of the Self by the self, but it is uncertain which "self" is the subject of "chooses" (*vr̥ṇute*, √*vr̥*, meaning also to "woo") in the third line. We assume, with most of the translators, that *eṣa* refers back to *ayam ātmā* (the Self) as subject. However this may be, the problem whether or not *eṣa vr̥ṇute* implies a "doctrine of Divine Grace and . . . personal God" (Rawson) does not depend on the grammar here. If we regard the choice or wooing of the lower principle by the higher as an "act of grace", then it goes without saying that a doctrine of "Grace" and a sense of personal relationship with the divine Eros had been taught and felt long before the time of KU. Nor is there any opposition between the doctrines of a personal and an impersonal deity: "personal *and* impersonal" (*pauruṣyāpauruṣya*) — like *śabdāśabda, kālākāla, parimitāparimita,* etc. — is only one of the many ways of describing the divine *dvaitībhāva.*

In this connection it must not be overlooked that a doctrine of Grace implies also one of Disgrace: "He causes him whom he wishes to lead up from these worlds to perform right acts, and whom he wishes to lead downwards to perform unright acts"(Kauṣ U. III.8. cf. Heracleitus, Fr. XLIV). If this appears to deny our moral responsibility (the *akiriyavāda* heresy, attributed also to the Amaurians, see HJAS IV.119f., and cf. St. Augustine, *De spir. et lit.* 60), the answer is that the freedom of choice is ours to ask what boon we will (*varaṁ vr̥ṇita yaṁ kāmaṁ kāmayeta tam*) and that whoever prays sincerely in the words of the "elevation" (*abhyāroha*), "Lead me from what is naughty to what is aughty (*asato mā sad gamaya*), from darkness to light, from death to immortality" assuredly obtains his desire (BU I.3.28). In other words, the Lord bestows his grace on those who "choose" his leading, and "disgraces" those who do not seek it. In the same way the king may or may not "choose" the guidance of a qualified *purohita*: in our text it is clear that the choice has been made, and the spoken words are those of the *purohita* expressing his acceptance of the king whom he will "cause to perform right acts", and therefore to prosper.

70. In *Heres* 258, Philo calls Sarah the *ek physeōs archousan aretēn* and in *Abr.* 99 Philo takes *arete* masculine to *logismos* feminine.

71. Cf. TS I.6.7.4 "The sacrificer is a bolt (*vajra*), the enemy (*bhrātṛvyam*) of man is want (*kṣudram*); in that he fasts and does not eat, he straightway smites with a bolt, the enemy, want"; similarly II.5.6.6.

72. In an analysis of the ruling passions of the various human kinds or castes in A III.363 it is interesting to compare those attributed to the kṣatriya with those attributed to women: both lists of qualities end in the same way, "his vocation is to rule" (*issariya pariyosāna,* over which Sirī presides, *Jātaka* no. 382), and "her vocation is to rule". The word *pariyosāna* (Skr. *pari-ava-syu*) almost literally "tie-up" or "connection", means vocation, function, entelechy, goal, as may be seen from the fact that in the same context the Samaṇā's *Pariyosāna* is *nibbāna,* and the householder's (whose "support is an art") is "perfected work". It is not meant that it is the kṣatriya's and woman's mere *ambition* to rule, but that it pertains to them to do so. In other words, the characteristically royal and feminine function is that of *administration;* the one administering a kingdom, the other a household (cf. Proverbs, XXXI.10f.). "Administration" implies, of course, the presence of another and authoritative principle, on behalf of which the "administrator" acts. It is well known that the Indian woman, in fact, "rules" the house.

There is another way in which the king and the woman correspond: both are "devoted". We have already seen that the king's patronage of the brāhmaṇa corresponds to Indra's bestowal of his "share" (*bhāgam,* ṚV VIII.100.1; cf. n. 6) on Agni, and that this offering makes the king a *bhaktā;* it is in the same way that the wife offers his share of the meal to her husband before partaking of what is left, the remains of her sacrifice. It would be as "incorrect" for her to eat with him as it would be for the king to eat with his *purohita.*

It is by no means an accident, or merely historical "development" that "the doctrine of *bhakti* should have been so little emphasized in the Upaniṣads and so much in BG. For it is the Way of Gnosis (*jñāna-mārga*) that pertains to the Brāhman, and the emotional Way of Devotion (*bhakti-mārga*), which is also a Way of Sacrificial Action (*karma-mārga*), that pertains to the king. The relation of a vassal to a feudal lord, which is also that of the Regnum to the Sacerdotium, is essentially one of "loyalty" (a word that better than "devotion", perhaps, conveys the meaning of *bhakti*), and that is precisely the relation of the woman to the man, her "lord"; there is a real equivalence of the Japanese *harakiri* and the Indian *satī*, and it is in the same way that the "soul" (always f.) must "put itself to death" for the sake of the spirit to which it owes allegiance.

We can see all this as clearly in the connection of European Chivalry (*kṛatram*) with a devotional mysticism, and in the corresponding Ṣūfī devotional literature, with its "Fidèles de l'Amour", as in India. As has been pointed out by René Guénon, "Nous ne pouvons que singaler . . . le rôle important que joue le plus souvent un élement fēminin, ou représenté symboliquement comme tel, dans les doctrines des Kshatriyas. . . . Ce fait peut s'expliquer, d'une part, par la préponderance de l'élément 'rajasique' et émotif chez les Kshatriyas, et surtout, d'autre part, par la correspondence du féminin, dans l'orde cosmique, avec Prakriti ou 'La Nature primordiale', principle du devenir et de la mutation temporelle." (*Autorité spirituelle et Pouvoir temporel,* 1930, p. 93, n. 1).

"We must point out . . . the important role frequently played by a feminine element, or an element symbolically represented as such in the doctrines of the kṣatriyas. . . . This fact may be explained, on the one hand, by a preponderance of the 'rājasic' or emotional element in the kṣatriyas, and, on the other hand (and most of all), by the correspondence of the feminine, in the cosmic order, with Prakṛti or 'primordial Nature', the principle of becoming and of temporal mutation". (*Spiritual Authority and Temporal Power,* by René Guénon, 1930, p. 93, n. 1).

The Sacerdotium and the man are the intellectual, and the Regnum and the woman the active elements in what should be literally a symphony. Over against the intellectuality and continence that are proper in the former the emotional and erotic qualities of the latter are in due proportion, necessary and indispensable to society; for without the softer woof to be combined with the harder weft, the social tissue could not be woven at all. But it must also be realized that in any normal decadence (such as that of the last centuries in Europe), the progressive "emancipation" of the less intellectual and more emotional elements in the community will mean the gradual substitution of feeling for knowing as a basis for judgement in conduct or art. In ethics, the notion of altruism will take the place of that of justice; in literature, words will more and more be used for their emotive effect than treated as the vehicle of thought. We ultimately reach just such a condition of sentimentality as is characteristic of modern societies; and it need hardly be pointed out that if the social tissue is to be woven entirely of the softer elements, it cannot be expected to wear well.

73. For the marriage of Sky and Earth, see Aeschylus, Loeb classical Library, ed. II.395.

74. "O Agni, the wise one, do thou avert for us the anger of Varuṇa, the God" (R̥V IV.1.4, TS II.5.12.3); "May he (Agni) save us from the overwhelming duress, the curse, the overwhelming wrong . . . from Varuṇa's craft" (R̥V I.128.5-7); Thou, Agni, hast freed the gods from their curse" (R̥V VII.13.2), and similar texts. By the same token, Br̥haspati is the "remitter of debts".

75. JB III.200 "The gods to whom no offering is made do not eat": PB XIV.6.8 (Indra addressing Kutsa) "Offer a sacrifice to me, for I am hungry".

As Keith has pointed out (HOS XXXI.259) the basis of the sacrifice is an exchange of gifts. We find the sacrificer saying: "Give thou to me; I shall give to thee. . . . Accept my offering, I shall accept thy offering" (TS I.8.4.1), and "with what goods (*dhánena*) I barter, seeking goods with goods, may that become more for me, not less" (AV III.15.5-6); "What the sacrificer does for the gods here, that they do for him there" JU I.233); "Indra does not rob his worshipper, but returns his gifts more abundantly" (R̥V VI.28.2), cf. AV III.15.1 where Indra is called a "trader" (*vaṇijam*) and as such contrasted with the "miser" (*árātim*). This is, indeed, a *commerce* of man with God, but in the primary sense of the word, that of establishing personal relationships (Webster, 2), rather than in that of our modern "business". Even today the Indian shopkeeper is apt to ask: "Do you think I am in business only for *profit*?" The transaction is paralleled in the lavish exchanges of useful gifts which we meet with as a worldwide practise in "primitive" societies where, at the same time that the actual benefits of a "trade" are secured, the main purpose is that of the cementing of friendly and reciprocal relations. An enduring friendship, all on one side and without reciprocity of any kind, would be unreal.

The commerce of the *Do ut des* texts is, moreover, identical with that implied by the term *bhakti* = *bhāga*, literally "share" or "portion", from √*bhaj* to "apportion". Thus in R̥V X.51.8 Agni only consents to conduct the sacrifice on condition of receiving his "portion" of the oblation (*haviṣo datta bhāgám*), cf. II.10.6 where the sacrificer thinks of himself as winning "wealth" (*dhanasāḥ*) by his invocation. As we have seen (n. 6, q.v.), and as is also evident from the fact that the sacrificial commerce is really an exchange of wedding gifts, the implied agreement or mutual understanding (*saṁjñāna*) has as much to do with love as with advantage. A man does not "love" his wife the less because he "provides for" her and she "serves" him or his, as we are God's, to "love, honour and obey him". It is the same in feudal relations, where the "devotion" of thane to Earl (as in *Beowulf*) is of just the same sort as that of the woman to the man or the man to God. If love be literally a "lik(en)ing", we cannot really love anyone, other than one whose will we do, or one who does our will.

The Sacrifice is a "devotion", and that is as much as to say a self-sacrifice; and in fact, while the God is archetypally the victim, in the ritual mimesis the sacrificer identifies himself with the actual victim, as is often explicit: "the fire knows that he has come to give himself to me" (*paridām me*, ŚB II.4.1, 11, cf. IX.3.2.7 *yajñó vai devánām ātmá, yajñá u evá yājamānasya*), and hence the distinction of the "self-sacrificer" (*ātmayāji*) from the mere "sacrificer", ŚB XI.2.6.13.14, cf. Eggeling's note on ŚB I.2.3.5. In the last analysis, the Sacrificer is exchanging or, if we prefer to say so, "bartering" his own eye for the Sun's, his own for the divine substance. (*Mathnawī* I.922 "His eye for ours, what a goodly recompense!".)

The language of commerce, in fact, survives in the most characteristically devotional contexts, for example in Mīrā Bāī's well-known song:

Kāṅh have I bought. The price he asked, I gave.
Some cry, " 'Tis great", and others jeer " 'Tis small" —
I gave in full, weighed to the utmost grain,
My love, my life, my self, my soul, my all.

It would be very difficult to show that it was in any other spirit that the sacrificer made himself over to Agni. It is only our own bias that stands in the way of a realization of the real content. If the virtue of self-sacrifice is, no more than any other virtue, "its own reward" but is with a view to results ("Thine may we be, for thee to give us treasure", ṚV II.2.1), the last end in view being that of a rebirth from the Fire in an immortal body of glory, this consciousness of ends, whether here or hereafter (metaphysical rites have always in view to secure both of these ends), no more implies a "loveless" relationship than does a feudal or marital "contract".

We must not be distracted from a realization of this by the unquestionable fact that, as Keith has rightly pointed out, the sacrificial gift is by no means a thank-offering, or by the fact that there is no word in Hindi for "thanks". The Indian point of view is that we do not say "thanks"; we do something about it. The beggar who receives alms offers no thanks; he has favoured the giver with an opportunity to be generous. The whole stress, indeed, is upon the aristocratic virtue of generosity, not on the servile expression of gratitude. Our notion that "Virtue is its own reward", so far from being admirable, is only the expression of a cynical disbelief in an ultimate order and justice, a distrust in man's or God's magnanimity. In all interpretation of the Vedic Sacrifice by European scholars there must always be discounted their (often unconscious) anti-traditional, and especially anti-feudal and anti-clerical, prejudices.

76. Caland, in annotation of PB VII.10.3 renders *dhūmam* by "fog" and so misses the whole point. It is because all gifts are essentially sacrifices that "A gift is given with the words 'This is smoke'" (JUB I.58.6 and CU V.8). Nothing more profound than this has ever been said about giving.

    Cf. JB III.216 — Ascent of oblation, descent of rain dependent on performance of sacrifice: when omitted, gods and men *both* hunger. See also AB IV.27, ŚB VII.3.1.29-30, ŚB IX.4.4.3.

77. "It is upon the observance of ritual that the governance of a State depends" (Confucius, *Analects*, XI.25). "Wherever the idea of divine kingship prevails we find coupled with it the conviction that upon the correct performance of kingly ritual depends the whole welfare of the State, the fertility of its lands, the fruitfulness of its trees, the fecundity both of its women and of its herds and flocks". (Waley, *The Analects of Confucius*, p. 65; *Odyssey* XIX.109f; A.C.L. Brown, *Grail Legend*, p. 133; Chrétien, vs. 4679). Waley further points out that the "power that enabled Divine Kings to deal with all things under Heaven" depended not only upon the correct performance of the rites but also upon an understanding of them; this is just as it is in the Indian texts where it is only to the comprehensor (*evamvit; ya evam veda*) that the ultimate benefits of any given rite really accrue.

78. In ŚB IX.3.2.1 and 4 the shower of wealth (*vasordhārā*) is both "Agni's shower" inasmuch as he is the Vasu, and also the "shower

of Wealth" with which he is aspersed (*abhiṣikta*) as Emperor. ŚB IX.3.3.15-19 explains its nature: "Its self or body (*ātman*) is the sky, the cloud its udder, lightning its teat, the shower the shower (of rain); from the sky it comes to the cow (i.e. from the sky as archetypal cow to the earthly cow, so that on earth), its self or body is the cow . . . its shower the shower (of milk); and from the cow it comes to the sacrificer. He (in turn) is its self or body, his arm its udder, the offering ladle its teat, the shower (of *ghī*). From the sacrificer to the gods; from the gods to the cow; from the cow to the sacrificer; thus circulates this perpetual, never ending food of the gods. And, verily, whosoever is a comprehensor thereof, for him shall there be thus this perpetual never-ending Food" (the Bread of Life). See also TS V.4.8 and 7.3., and IV.7.1.

This same "circulation" is more briefly formulated in BG III.10-14; the successive terms of the endless series being *karman* (acts of the sacrificer), *yañja* (the sacrifice), *parjanya* (rain), *bhūtāni* (creatures), *anna* (food), and then again *karman,* and so without end. In MU VI.37 the application is made to the interior sacrifice: here the rain from above is the Chant (*udgītha*) "whereby living beings here on earth live".

Thus again we find that the performance of the sacrifice is the basis of the prosperity of the realm: it is from this point of view that in Mbh (Vana Parva, XXV) Bhīma addresses a king with the words, "Thy hand can rain gold". The source is inexhaustible; but the stream is not a stagnant one, only by the sacrifice can it be kept in circulation.

The *vasordhārā* doctrine outlined above explains the iconography of the series of representations of the *cakravartin* emperor at Amarāvatī, of which I republished several in an article entitled "A Royal Gesture" in the *Feestbundel v.d.K. Bataviaasch Genootschap van Kunsten en Wetenschapen,* Weltevreden, Pt. 1, 1929; and republished here as Frontispiece. In these representations the Cakravartin, surrounded by his "Seven Treasures", is raising his right arm to the clouds, from which a shower of coins, i.e. "wealth", *vasu*) is falling. It is manifest that the emperor's hand is the "ladle" of the Sacrifice, and that it is raised in accordance with ŚB VII.2.3.9 where the offering of *ghī* is fivefold, to agree with the five strata of the altar and "when he offers, he raises (the ladle) and so builds Agni up with his five strata". Cf. Dh.186 *Kahapaṇavarsa* and JB III.216.

However T.N. Ramachandran in *Papers published by the Rao Sahib G.V. Ramamurthi Pantalu's Birthday Celebration Committee* connects the Cakravartin types of Amarāvatī, Jagayyapeṭa and Goli with the Māndhātu Jātaka.

79. Unlike Agni, the Sacerdotium, "not vain-glorious because of his Counsel" (*kratvā . . . apradṛpitaḥ*, ṚV I.145.2).

80. All political systems which directly contravene the law of nature and the liberties of the spiritual power, are necessarily short-lived" (George Avery, SSM., in *New English Weekly*, 25 July 1940). "Division between Church and Lay, that is what shall subsist now. . . . Church shall be enslaved by State . . . evil shall overtake the State. . . . By perfidy of all men the fruits of the earth shall perish, the mast of trees and the produce of the waters" (from the interpretation of Dermot's dream, Standish H.O'Grady, *Silva Gadelica*, II, p. 84). "Verily, so long as Indra knew not that Self, so long the Titans overcame him. . . . When he knew, then striking down and conquering the Titans, he compassed the chieftaincy, autonomous rule and overlordship of all gods and all beings" (Kauṣ. U. IV.20). In Platonic terms, there can be no stability where there is no agreement as to which shall rule, the better or the worse part. "Every kingdom divided against itself is brought to a desolation" (Luke XI.17).

81. AV X.2.30 — *puraṁ yo brahmaṇo veda yasyāḥ puruṣa ucyate.* He who knows the fullness of Brahma, from which (fullness) He is called *puruṣa*; BU II.5.18 — *sa vā ayaṁ puruṣaḥ sarvāṁsu pūrṣu puriṣayaḥ* = He on account of his dwelling in all bodies is called the Puruṣa.

82. Most Chinese philosophic schools have taught the way of what is called the "Inner Sage and Outer King". The Inner Sage is a person who has established virtue in himself: the Outer King is one who has accomplished great deeds in the world. The highest ideal for a man is at once to possess the virtue of a Sage and the accomplishment of a Ruler, and so become what is called a Sage-king (Janaka), or what Plato would term the Philosopher-king" (Fung Yu-lan, *History of Chinese Philosophy;* tr. Derk Bodde, Peiping, 1937, p. 2). The Inner Sage, the *prajñātman*, is the emperor, or King of kings, the *jīvātman* the Viceroy, and it is for the latter and active self to do what the former and contemplative self enjoins, not to "do as he likes".

83. *Republic* 432 C, etc. Plato's doctrine of the individual "city" is exactly paralleled in the Indian *brahmapura* (City of God) contexts. For example, "(This body) with its eight 'circles' and nine apertures is Ayodhyā ['unconquerable'], the City of the Gods, its golden treasury [heart] enfolded by the light of heaven; he who is a comprehensor of that city of Brahma, by immortality enfolded, him Brahma and Brahmā (Comm. Paramātman and Prajāpati) dower with life, renown and progeny" (AV X.2.29-31). The Purī and Mathurā is in every man, the kingdom of his own mind, where the personal self is to be *put down . . . the* Kaṁsa in each of us" (P.N. Sinha, *A Study of the Bhāgavata Purāṇa,* 1901, p. 300). "One who has slain his Vṛtra" (TS II.5.4.5) has done this.

84. The distinction of births in JB I.17 corresponds exactly to that of John III.6 " *That which is born of the flesh is flesh; and that which is born of the Spirit is spirit"*, and Gal. VI.8 *"For he that soweth to his flesh shall of the flesh reap corruption; but he that soweth to the Spirit shall of the Spirit reap life everlasting"*.

The "two selves" of the Sanskrit texts, Plato's "mortal and immortal parts of the soul", are the Outer and Inner Man, *that which is outward* and *that which is inward,* of II Cor. IV.16: of which St. Thomas Aquinas remarks *"In man are two natures* (an echo of Plato's *duo phamen auto anagkaion einai, Republic* 604b — two distinct principles in man), *his spiritual nature and his corporeal nature. And a man is said to love himself by reason of his loving himself with regard to his spiritual nature* (Sum. Theol. II.26.4, as in BU IV.5.6, etc.). See also Aristotle on "self-love".

It is with reference to the corporeal self or "life" — the Buddhist "petty self" (*appātumo*) "which is not my (real) self" *na me so ātta, passim* — that Christ says *"If any man come to me, and hate not . . . his own life also, he cannot be my disciple"* (Luke XIV.26), and with reference to their division Plato's katharsis, the "separating of soul from body, so far as that is possible", *Phaedo* 67c) that St. Paul affirms that the Word of God (sc. all *śruti*) extends to the sundering of soul from spirit (Heb. IV.12). The distinction is that which is drawn by Philo (*Quaestiones in Genesis,* II.59 and *De Cherub*. 113f., as cited by Goodenough, *By Light, Light,* pp. 374, 375) between "us" and "that which was before our birth" and will be (cf. BG II.12) "when we, who in our junction with our bodies, are mixtures, shall not exist, but shall be brought into the rebirth", i.e. "born again" of the

Divine Womb in the sense of JB I.17 and John III.3.

The "two selves" are, again, the *proprium* and the *suum* (*le moi* and *le soi*) of St. Bernard. We "naturally" identify "ourselves" with the *proprium*, "our" individuality as known by "name and aspect" (*nāma rūpa*), "this man" to which we return from the sacrificial deification thinking: "Now am I he who I really am" (*aháṁ yá evásmi sāsmi*, ŚB I.9.3.23), and to which the king returns with the same words at the end of the Rajasuya in which he had been made a brāhmaṇa (AB VII.24); which coming back to one self are in the most technical sense of the word "desecrations". In thus returning we are forgetting that the *proprium* to which we return is not our real Self, not really an essence at all, but only a process. It is, on the other hand, with reference to our essence, St. Bernard's *suum*, that it is said "That art thou" (CU VI.8.7f.), and with reference to that Self "the Overlord and king of all beings (BU II.5.15), that the Oracle enjoins, γνῶθι σεαυτόν (*gnōthi seauton*). When Philosophia enquires of Boethius what he is, and he answers "a reasoning and mortal animal", she tells him that he has "forgotten" who he is and warns him: "If thou knowest not thyself, depart" (*Deconsol.*, prose vi and *Cant.* I.8).

The injunction "Know thyself" is paralleled in the questions of the Brāhmaṇas and Upaniṣads, "Which self?" (*kataraḥ sa ātmā*, AA II.6; *katamá ātmā* BU IV.3.7, MU II.I; and similarly *ken 'attanā*, S. 508) and "In whom, when I go forth hence, shall I be going forth?" (*kasmin . . . utkrānto bhaviṣyāmī*, Praśna U. VI.3) with the answer in CU III.14.4 "in Brahma". The true answer to the question "who art thou?" (*kas tvam asi*), viz. "what thou art, that light am I" (*ko 'ham asmi suvas tvam*), is the password that opens the gates of the kingdom of Heaven and wins the welcome "Come in, O myself" (JUB III.14.1-5; Kauṣ. U. I.5-6; Rūmī, *Mathnawī*, I.3062 f.). Incidentally, I am convinced that the Delphic γνῶθι σεαυτόν (*gnōthi seauton*) and E are a question (*signum*) and an answer (*responsum*) asked and given at the door (certainly a "Sundoor") of Apollo's shrine; "Know thyself" implying "Who art thou", and E = EI meaning (1) Apollo and (2) "thou art" (these are two of Plutarch's interpretations, *Moralia* 392 A), the answer to the question "Who art thou" (seeking admittance) taking the form "The Sun thou art" (that am I). "'That thou art, thus may I be', he says in effect. . . . Verily, he invokes this blessing" (TS I.5.7.6) cf. my "The 'E' at Delphi" in *Review of Religion*, November 1941.

85. Hence in order to reach their source "Both *vidyā* and *avidyā* are to be understood" (*vidyāṁ ca avidyāṁ ca yastad vedôbhayaṁ saḥ . . . amṛtam āsnute*, Īśa Up. 11. The world of pairs of opposites, affirmations and negations, good *and* evil, is a theophany. It has not been said that "the invisible things of him" (Rom. I.20) are only to be known by those of the things that were made that seem to *us* "good"; the obvious answer to the question "Did he who made the lamb make thee?" is affirmative. The problem of evil ("Can a good God have permitted this?", cf. JUB I.18.2) can only be posed by a monophysite or a dualist. The Muslim sees in Heaven and Hell the "reflections" of the divine Mercy (Sacerdotium) and divine Majesty (Regnum), cf. *Mathnawī* I.1128, 1298, Nicholson's *Mystics of Islam*, p. 98, Goodenough, Philo.

In That One (*tad ekam, ekam aviviktam, viśvam ekam, advaitam, ekatvam*) Mitra and Varuṇa male and female, lamb and lion "lie down together". To praise or blame Him for the existence of any one of these pairs is to praise or blame Him for that of the other, because each presupposes the other, to praise or blame Him for making a world at all, for a world-picture (of love-joy) can only be painted in chiaroscuro, not all in white or all in black. Yet it is *our* ends that the world of good and evil serves, for without it there would be no way of procedure from potentiality to act. It is not the First Cause, but *our* knowledge of good *and* evil that is the occasion of our mortality (cf. *Chain of Being*). This First Cause, which we cannot call either good or evil in any human sense, is the cause of our existence, but we ourselves are the cause of our manner of being.

It does not follow that the distinction of good from evil and truth from falsehood lacks validity here and now, as though both could be called good. The way to the Unity of Brahma leads from the Darkness, Untruth, and Death to the Light, Reality, and Life (BU I.3.8): it was by following this "Ancient Path" (ṚV IV.18.1, BU IV.4.8, S. II.106, IV. 117, etc.) that the Devas separated themselves from the Asuras and became what they are (ŚB IX.5.1.12)", "by qualification" (*arháṇā*) that they (who with exception of Agni were originally mortal) became immortals (ṚV X.63.4), assimilated to him "whose name is Truth" (CU VIII.3.4, I John V.20, etc.). By this *via affirmativa* one rises higher and higher in the hierarchy of degrees of reality or truth (MU IV.6) until we reach the Sun, who is the Truth absolutely (JUB I.5.3 and *passim*) but *through* whom the way leads on to Brahma; to reach that Unity, the ultimate reality that was hidden by the Truth" (BU I.6.3), we must deny the names that have been given to God, to know him only as unknown (MU IV.6, Kena Up. II.3). In other words, the end of the road (*adhvanaḥ pāram*) and summit of contingent being (*bhavāgra*) bring us to a wall through which the only way is by the strait gate of the Sundoor, that bars the way to anyone who still is anyone (Cuṣa, *De Visione Dei*, IX, fin). What lies beyond is "other than Law or lack of Law, other than our well or ill-done, other than past or future" (*anyatra dharmād anyatrādharmād anyatrāsmāt kṛtākṛtāt anyatra bhūtāc ca bhavyāc ca*, KU II.14; there, as Eckhart expresses it, "neither vice nor virtue ever entered in" to Him who is "neither good nor true". St. Thomas, *Sum. Theol.* I.46.1 ad 3 — *omne quod generatur, generatur ex contrario* = from its opposite, *not* "contradictories"; if based on *Phaedo* 70E does not mean *pairs* of opposites but from its opposite, *Phaedo* 71A — *panta ostō, gignetai, ex enantiōn ta enantia pragmata.*

86. See n. 47. Just as in Christianity, all creation is feminine to God, and in the same way, the body feminine to the Spirit. All birth depends upon the conjugation (*saṁyoga*) of the "Knower of the Field" with the "Field" (BG XIII); as a wife to a husband, so is the body (*tanu*), which is for the sake of good works (*sukṛtāya kam*), to the Spirit (*ātman*, TS I.1.10.1-2); the Sun is our real Father (JUB III.10.4 and ṚV X.149.4 *patiriva jāyāmabhi no nyetu dhartā divaḥ savitā viśvavāraḥ*). All this must be taken for granted if the theory of government is to be understood.

    It may be added that there is nothing so strange about the relation of Kṛṣṇa to the *gopīs*, his *bhaktas*, as is often supposed: Peter Sterry, for example, writes "*The Lord* Jesus *hath* his Concubines, *his* Queenes, *his Virgines, Saints* in Remoter *Formes, Saints* in higher *Formes, Saints* unmarried *to any Forme*, who keep themselves single for the immediate imbraces of their Love" (Vivian da Sola Pinto, *Peter Sterry, Puritan and Platonist*, p. 25). It should be noted that these are the words of a *Puritan* divine.

    Irenaeus (I.13.3) quotes the gnostic Markos, "Prepare thyself as a bride to receive a bridegroom, that thou mayest be what I am and I what thou art", cf. VS VIII.10 *agne vākpatim.*

87. The passage is pertinent both to the story of Indra's enlightenment (CU VIII.7-11) and to that of his fall and apokatastasis (BD VII.54f.).

88. Plato recognizes two kinds or parts of the "soul" in us, or two lives or selves, mortal and immortal; with one or the other of these we identify "ourselves". The man governed by his desires is (*ēttōn heautou*), "subject to himself", i.e. to the self that says "I want"; one who governs his desires is (*creitton heautou*), i.e. "master of himself", i.e. of the self that says "I want" (*Laws* 645, *Republic* 431, etc). In the first case he (the subject predicated by *ēttōn* and κρείττων *creitton*) identifies "himself" with the *śarīra ātman* (*bhūtātman*), "overcome" by likes and dislikes (MU III.2), in the second case with the imperturbable *aśarīra ātman* (*prajñātman*). The former condition is one of "ignorance", *avidyā*) the latter one of "wisdom" (*vidyā*) (*Protagoras* 358). The welfare of the "whole soul" depends upon the harmony of its parts and their "unanimity as to which shall rule" (*Republic* 432 c). All this is the same for the State and in the individual economy.

89. Cf. Muṇḍ. Up. III.1.4. The language is equally applicable to the political economy of Regnum and Sacerdotium, and to the individual economy of the "two selves", Outer King and Inner Sage.

    For the *kāmācārin* cf. R̥V IX.113.9; JUB III.28.3; CU VIII.5.4; Taitt. U. III.5; D. I.172; John X.9; and HJAS IV, 1939, p. 35.

    As it is primarily the Gale of the Spirt that "moveth as it will" (*yathāvaśam*, R̥V X.168.4; *anilo viya yathā kāmaṁ*, J V. 418; John III.8), so it is only one "gone with the wind" (Kauṣ U. II.12, etc.) in the sense of the requiem *gacchatu vātam ātma* (R̥V X.16.3) that can be called "free"; or to use the language of NT, only those who are "in the spirit" (*pneumati*) that can "pass in and out".

90. Similarly the Buddhist D. I.172, forming part of the instruction of a King in the "Advantages of the Monastic Life": the servant of desire is his own slave, not his own master nor able to go where he will (*na yena kāmaṁ gamo = na kāmācārin*), while the man "the doors of whose senses are guarded (*indriyesu gutta-dvāro = atta-gutto*, Dh. 379) is his own master, freed from his slavery *dāsavyā mutto, asura* nature) and able to go where he will". In almost identical language Plato describes those who are "subject to themselves" (see n. 88) as "freeman only in name" (*Republic* 431C). He tells us also regarding the education of Persian princes, that they had four tutors, respectively most wise, most just, most temperate, and most brave. The first taught him the Magian lore* of Zoroaster, the second

* On the Magi, see Philo *Spec.* Loeb. Lib. 632f.

always to be truthful, the fourth to be fearless, and the third "not to be mastered even by a single pleasure, in order that he may acquire the habit of being a free and real King, one who is first of all the ruler of whatever (powers) are in himself, and not their slave" (*Alcibiades* I.122). We can readily believe that the Persian and Indian conceptions of kingship were indeed alike, cf. Cicero, *De Divinatione* I.91 — "Nor can anyone be king of the Persians who beforehand does not understand the greater discipline and science". And on the *Graal King*". See Philo, QE 105, Goodenough, p. 113.

91. The "free-will that Christian doctrine asserts for all is evidently not the "self-will", but rather a freedom to resist or consent to the higher will, that of the spirit ("the spirit is willing but the flesh is weak", Math. XXVI.41). To do our own will is to be passive; to co-operate with the spirit is to be in act, cf. n. 69. That the natural man is an automaton is admirably demonstrated in S. III.66-67 (see HJAS IV, 1939, p. 135).

92. *Samprayat,* to "proffer", correlative of *Vr̥* to "woo".

93. i.e. *paraṁ jyotirūpa sampadya svena rūpeṇa abhiniṣpadyante* (CU VIII.12.3).

94. AB VII.15, S. I.61-62, A II.48-49, see my "The Pilgrim's Way" in JBORS XXIII and XXIV, 1937, 1938.

95. Thomas Kempis, *The Imitation of Christ* III chap. XIII — "There is no worse, and no more grievous enemy to thy soul than thyself, if thine flesh be not well agreeing to the will of the spirit."

96. Cf. Walt Whitman — "My dinner, dress, associates, looks . . . the sickness of one of my folks or of myself, or ill doing or loss or lack of money, or depressions or exaltations . . . these come to me days and nights and go from me again. But they are not this Me myself. Apart from the pulling and hauling stands what I am. . . . Both in and out of the game and watching and wondering at it."

97. The whole of this symbolism recurs in Plato (*Phaedrus* 246, 247, etc.) and Hermes Trismegistus (I.11f., etc.).

98. How is the victory to be won in this *jehād?* Our self is the enemy (Die before you die), in its ignorance of and opposition to its self is the enemy to be convinced. The way is one of intellectual preparation, moral discipline, leading, and contemplation; in other words, at the same time a theory and a way of living.

The intellectual preparation is philosophical (the word), as "philosophy" was understood by the ancients. The proper object of philosophy in this sense is stated in the words of the Delphic oracle "Know thy Self" (*gnōthi seauton*).

99. Plato, "God is our guardian, and we are his possessions" (*Phaedo*, 60D).

100. An identical interpretation of "sleep" will be found in Hermes Trismegistus *Lib.* I.1. The Outer Man, whom we think of as "awake" is *really asleep* and dreaming; the Inner and contemplative Man whom we think of as "asleep" when we fail to understand the metaphysical "inaction" is *really awake* and in act, in the sense that the Buddha is literally the "Wake" and the anagogical (*paramārthika*) sense in which Agni is "wakened at daybreak" (*uṣar-budh*).

101. For the "person in the (right) eye" see BU IV.2.2-3 and IV.4.1, CU I.7.5, MU VII.11.1-3. This image seen in the pupil of the eye is the form of our real being and that of the "Person in the Sun" who is called variously Death, Breath, and usually Indra; the "Person in the Sun" being "Indra; Prajāpati, Brahma" (Sacerdotium) (KB VIII.3). In ŚB III.1.3.15 it is Śuṣṇa that becomes the pupil of the eye.

The symbolism of the "person seen in the eye" is probably ancient. Plato (*Alcibiades* I.133) uses it in a slightly different way, but for him also it is a form analogous to what in us is most like God.

102. *Aticchandā,* usually interpreted to mean "beyond desires", but really with more direct reference to the *chandāṅsi* which are the means of our metrical re-integration and the wings on which the Spirit ascends to the Sun (AV VIII.9.2, AB VII.27, etc.). "Yonder Sun is the Disposer; and it is inasmuch as he hath gone unto the uttermost of the Quarters that there he stands and glows. . . . The Metres are the Quarters" (*diśo hy ètāś chándāṅsi,* ŚB IX.5.1.37, 39). *Átichandá* (for *átichandam*) in BU IV.3.21 is, according to Śaṅkara, beyond desires"; but I think that the reference is to the "whole and complete" form, like that of the fire-altar, *átichandās* in ŚB X.5.4.8, where the meaning of the word is certainly "hypermetrical" or "super-metrical". So in TS V.3.8.3 –– "all the metres are the Atichandas; verily he piles it with all the metres. The Atichandas is the highest of the metres. . . ".

103. "In the embrace of this sovran one which naughts the separated self of things, being is one without distinction. . . . One and one

uniting, void shines into void . . . so does the soul in God turn into God". Eckhart, English tr. of Pfeiffer's version by C. de B. Evans, I, pp. 368, 380.

104. On the Synteresis (essentially the same as Plato's immanent *logos daimon,* and *hēgemōn,* and/or "con-science" but with far more than the merely moral values that this latter word now implies for us) see O. Renz. *The Synteresis nach dem heiligen Thomas von Aquin* Münster, 1911. "Synteresis" is etymologically Skr. *saṁtāraka* √*tṝ*), "One who enables another to cross over" (to the farther shore), and so "saviour" or "deliverer".

105. For this expression see Masson-Oursel, "Une connexion dans l'esthétique de la philosophie de l'Inde, *Revue des Arts Asiatiques* II, 1925. "A connection in the aesthetics of Indian Philosophy."

106. The *indriyāṇī* are the five organs of sense, the five corresponding internal faculties, and the mind (*manas*); these correspond to what are called by Christian writers the "powers of the soul". They are properly called *indriyāṇī* because of their belonging to Indra, whose they are (cf. TS I.6.12.1, ŚB VI.1.1.2). They are, in fact, the "powers" (*śácīḥ*) by which Indra is "empowered" (*śacivat*) and is the "Lord of power" (*śacīḥ*) as he is of Indrāṇī (*indrāṇīm pátiḥ,* ṚV X.86.11.12). Taken together, the *śacīḥ* and Śaci; the *indriyāṇī,* the powers of the soul, the soul herself. The marriage of Indra and Indrāṇī is that of the Sun and Moon, Eros and Psyche.

Rightly curbed, the *indriyāṇī* are "powers of rule", but allowed full rein, are the "ruling passions" to which we are subjected.

"The place of rulers is held by those who exercise authority over the sense". — Philo, *De Agricultura,* 58.

107. Apollonius, *Epistle and Valerium — archōn aristos, ho an hautou proteron archē.*

Bonaventura, *De Donae Sancto Spirito,* IV.10, t.v. p. 475 — "No one can have an ordered household unless he himself is ordered. If anyone wishes to have chaste servants, and he himself be not chaste, it cannot be". See also *Chuang Tzu,* p. 148; Behmen, *Supersensual Life,* p. 229, and Marcus Aurelius 14-15, on "Self-government".

108. *kṛtsnaṁ hi śāstram idam indriya-jayaḥ.*

The concept of "Victory" is of the utmost importance in the traditional theory or Kingship. Exoterically it is by an actual or implied victory over others that a King obtains the throne, but esoterically he is the true Victor who subdues his own passions, allying himself with the Self against himself. In Islam this becomes the concept of the "Holy War" (*jihād*) as distinguished from mere wars of conquest. The "heroism" (*vīrya, andreia*) expected of the Knight (kṣatriya), whether as King or as the Mortal Soul and Outer Man, is then no longer a matter of merely physical courage (such as animals-also possess), but a symbol and evidence of self-conquest and self-knowledge; autonomy, as we have seen, being the outward tally of an inward Self-control. Whoever has thus found Himself is necessarily both fearless and "invulnerable" (AV X.8.44, BG II, etc.). When the martyr says: "I have fought the good fight", this good fight is the Holy War. This does not mean that the two wars must be separately fought; the man-at-arms may be waging a war that is humanly speaking "just", and, if he be a Comprehensor, at the same time one that is "holy". In the latter case the battle itself becomes a sacrificial rite. It is in this way that it can be said of War that "Some he has marked out to be gods, and some to be men, some to be enslaved and some to be set free" (Heracleitus, Fr. XLIV). It is one thing to be "free" to do what one likes; only to have the "victory over pleasures" (*hē tōn hēdonōn nikē*) Plato, *Laws* 840 C is to be really free.

It is clear from the great king Aśoka's thirteenth edict that he had understood the real meaning of "Victory"; for after recounting his political victories and expressing his deep regret for them, because of the suffering inflicted on the conquered, he continues (line 7), "And this is the foremost Victory, the Victory of the Dharma"; while (lines 10-11) he enjoins upon his successors to "regard as 'Victory' the Victory of the Dharma, which avails for this world and the other".

In the beginning, it was the Brahma-Yakṣa that won the Victory (over the Asuras) for the Devas, and it is asked: "Can he be conquered who is a comprehensor of that great first-born Yakṣa, who knows that Brahma to be the Truth?" (TS VI.5.7.4, JUB IV.21, Kena Up. III.1f., etc).

109. "What is the best thing of all for a man, that he may ask from the gods? 'That he may be always at peace with himself'."

— *Contest of Homer and Hesiod*, 320

Works noted in A.K. Coomaraswamy's copy of the First Edition as additional references

Aiyangar, K.V. Rangaswami, *Rajadharma,* Madras, 1941.

Buckler, F.W., *Epiphany of the Cross,* 1938.

———, *Firdausī's Shāhnāmah and the Geneologia Regni Dei,* Supplement to the *JAOS,* no. 1, 1935.

Comfort, W.W., *Chretien de Troyes,* Everyman's Libray.

Dennett, R.E., *At the Back of the Black Man's Mind,* 1906.

Engnell, I., *Studies in Divine Kingship: The Ancient Near East,* Uppsala, 1943.

Fennell, C.A.M., *Pindar,* 1899.

Figgis, J.N., *The Theory of the Divine Right of Kings,* CUP, 1896.

Gaster, T.H., *Divim Kingship in the Ancient Near East,* Review of Religion, vol. IX, 1945.

Gonda, J., *Ancient Indian Kinship from the Religious Point of View,* from NVMEN, vols. III, IV, 1966, Brill, Leiden.

Goodenough, E.R., *An Introduction to Philo Judaeus,* 1940.

———, *Hellenistic Kingship,* Yale Classical Studies, I, 1928.

Hocart, A.M., *Kingship,* London, 1941.

———, *La Castes,* Paris, 1938.

———, *Caste: A Comparative Study,* London, 1950.

Mees, Gualtherus H., *Dharma and Society,* The Hague, 1935.

Shamaśāstry, R., *Kauṭilya's Arthaśāstra,* Mysore, 1951.